Knowing Who You Are

Knowing Who You Are

Eight Surprising Images of Christian Identity

MALCOLM J. GILL

Foreword by Mark Young

WIPF & STOCK · Eugene, Oregon

KNOWING WHO YOU ARE
Eight Surprising Images of Christian Identity

Copyright © 2015 Malcolm J. Gill. All rights reserved. Except for brief quotations in critical publications or reviews, no part of this book may be reproduced in any manner without prior written permission from the publisher. Write: Permissions, Wipf and Stock Publishers, 199 W. 8th Ave., Suite 3, Eugene, OR 97401.

Wipf & Stock
An Imprint of Wipf and Stock Publishers
199 W. 8th Ave., Suite 3
Eugene, OR 97401

www.wipfandstock.com

ISBN 13: 978-1-4982-1804-7

All Scripture quotations, unless otherwise indicated, are taken from the Holy Bible, New International Version®, NIV®. Copyright ©1973, 1978, 1984, 2011 by Biblica, Inc.™ Used by permission of Zondervan. All rights reserved worldwide. www.zondervan.com The "NIV" and "New International Version" are trademarks registered in the United States Patent and Trademark Office by Biblica, Inc.™

Scripture quotations marked (NLT) are taken from the *Holy Bible*, New Living Translation, copyright ©1996, 2004, 2007, 2013 by Tyndale House Foundation. Used by permission of Tyndale House Publishers, Inc., Carol Stream, Illinois 60188. All rights reserved.

Scripture quotations marked (ESV) are from the ESV® Bible (The Holy Bible, English Standard Version®), copyright © 2001 by Crossway, a publishing ministry of Good News Publishers. Used by permission. All rights reserved.

"Hast Thou No Scar?" from *Gold Cord: The Story of a Fellowship* by Amy Carmichael, © 1932 by The Dohnavur Fellowship. Used by permission of CLC Publications. May not be further reproduced. All rights reserved.

Manufactured in the U.S.A.

*For Tamara,
Annabel, Adam, and Zara*

With fond memories of our English adventure

Contents

Foreword by Mark Young | ix
Preface | xi
Acknowledgments | xiii

1 The Christian: What's in a Name? | 1
2 The Christian as Pilgrim | 14
3 The Christian as Citizen | 31
4 The Christian as Combatant | 47
5 The Christian as Farmer | 62
6 The Christian as Steward | 78
7 The Christian as Soldier | 95
8 The Christian as Laborer | 114
9 The Christian as Sheep | 130

Bibliography | 141

Foreword

As I PREPARED TO transition into my current position as the president of Denver Seminary, a friend gave me some simple, yet profound, advice: "Be yourself." Having been in the same role at another institution, he knew that the responsibilities are so broad and the expectations of others so unattainable, if you're not careful, you will find yourself trying to be what everyone else thinks you should be in order to do the job. The simplicity of the statement masks its importance. "Be yourself" demands that we live out our deepest convictions and values. It means that what matters to us the most is on full display as we set goals, make decisions, navigate relationships, and embrace the mission that God has given us.

You can't *be* who you are if you don't *know* who you are. That's why this book matters so much. In its pages you will find one of the most insightful and poignant explorations of our identity as Jesus-followers in print today. And how timely is that? The identity of those who confess Jesus as Lord is under duress. In the post-Christian West, the term "Christian" is so layered with the barnacles of two thousand years of institutional history that it means something far different than when it was first used of a community of Greeks and Jews who confessed Jesus as Messiah in Antioch in the mid first century.

The New Testament authors recognized the importance of creating a clear picture of the identity of believers in Jesus. They knew that the creation of an entirely new community, defined not by ethnicity or social status or economic level or profession but by religious confession, would generate suspicion and misunderstanding. Insults and slurs would follow. Persecution and even martyrdom awaited many of those who dared to defy social convention and join the ranks of Jesus-followers. In order to withstand the pressure to abandon their confession, believers needed to ground themselves in their true identity and hold fast to it so that they could fulfill the mission entrusted to them by the risen Christ. That's why

Foreword

we find such powerful metaphors of Christian identity in the pages of the New Testament.

In this book Malcolm Gill introduces us to eight of the images that the New Testament authors used to describe our identity. Here you'll encounter characters as diverse as a wanderer and a citizen, a fighter and a sheep, an executive and a laborer. Each metaphor is deeply embedded in the culture of the first century. Malcolm peels back the layers of cultural understanding and uncovers the essence of each image. He then transports them several worlds away and shows us how they all should make a difference in how we live as believers in the world today.

During a short visit to Poland, a country where we had lived for many years, my twelve-year-old son asked me a question that has echoed in my mind for decades, "Daddy, who am I?" Having spent most of his childhood in Poland, he was going through the whiplash of identity crisis after we had moved to the United States. Back in Poland he had felt completely at home. Yet he was also starting to feel at home with his new friends in the United States. "Daddy, who am I? Am I a Pole or an American?" Moistening eyes betrayed his sincerity. Instinctively, I answered him with these words, "You're a child of God."

Perhaps the best way to read this book is to begin with the simple prayer, "Lord, who am I?" and listen for his answer as you read.

Mark Young
President, Denver Seminary

Preface

I'M NOT NATURALLY A runner. Putting on a pair of jogging shoes, hitting the pavement, and grinding out a few miles are not activities that appeal to me at all. While I don't mind running if it involves chasing or kicking a ball, to simply jog for enjoyment's sake is something that I don't understand. In spite of my aversion to this activity, however, I've slowly realized that running can be helpful for one's general fitness. With this in mind, a little while ago I discovered a podcast that claimed it could help a person move from being relatively inactive to being one who could run five kilometers without stopping. I thought I'd give it a try.

On my first day, of this eight-week course, I began with vigor. The man on the podcast instructed me that I would run short bursts interspersed with periods of walking. Between the upbeat songs playing through my headphones a man's voice would sound out with encouraging remarks like, "just one minute more" and "keep going." It was difficult at first, but the weeks went by quickly and I began to run further and faster. I was developing a good level of fitness and feeling pretty good about things. Then, one day as I was halfway through the run my audio device ran out of battery. Only partially through the circuit I now found myself without music and more importantly I had no voice cheering me on and telling me that I could do it. The only thing I could hear were the sounds of my breath as I tried to huff and puff around the rest of the course. The end result, I quit running and walked home disconsolate.

There is something powerful about the encouragement of others when running. The words "you can do it" and "keep going" mean a lot when you want to give up and it is for this reason that I've written this book. I desperately want to finish the Christian race that is before me, and I want you to complete the race as well. When I began the journey of following Christ it felt as if I were in a large crowd with many fellow joggers beside me. Over the course of the years, however, I've noticed that a sizeable number of Christians who ran with me in the early days have given up and simply stopped pursuing Christ. Rather than running after their heavenly calling they have chosen to quit and follow their own desires.

As I look around at who is following Christ with me it is easy to be discouraged. A high proportion of friends that I grew up with in youth group have abandoned their commitment to Christ and currently live independently of him. I've known friends that I've studied with at seminary who at one time had great enthusiasm for the gospel yet later deserted their spouses and ministries in search of joy outside of Christ. I've witnessed countless congregational members who started the race well yet have lost interest and have forsaken Christ. Whereas when I started the Christian race I felt like I was in a marathon with a crowd of others, I now look around and at times feel there are only a few of us left who are striving toward Christ. It is often quite disheartening.

If you've ever felt discouraged, spiritually isolated, or even tempted to quit then I want to let you know that I've written this book to encourage you to keep running the Christian race. You're not alone, but as you know the road is narrow and difficult. In order to keep going we need the constant voice of encouragement to keep us moving in the right direction. The good news for us is that in the Scriptures we have a word of exhortation that propels us forward. The Bible aids us by providing focus, challenge, rebuke, and direction as we press on toward the goal to win the prize for which God has called us heavenward in Christ Jesus.

One of the ways the Bible helps us think about the Christian life is by providing a series of images from everyday life that reveals truth about our identity. Jesus, along with the New Testament authors, regularly used familiar metaphors in their teaching to illustrate what it meant to be a disciple of Christ. In this book I would like to explore eight lesser known images of Christian identity with the purpose that we might more fully understand what it means to be a follower of Jesus of Nazareth, and in doing so we may continue to mature into the likeness of our Master. Beginning with the origin of the term "Christian" and then moving on to explore select first-century images referenced in the New Testament the goal of this study is not to accumulate more information. Rather, it is to feel the weight of the comparative metaphors that we might *know who we are* in Christ and respond appropriately in our day-to-day following of him. So put on your running shoes, tie up your laces, and run with me as together we explore our Christian identity.

Acknowledgments

This book is the fruit of an enriching sabbatical spent at Tyndale House in Cambridge during the first half of 2014. I'm grateful for the wonderful fellowship extended to me while in Cambridge and in particular the support of Simon Sykes, Ferdie Mulder, Brad Green, Bruce Winter, Will Timmins, Ed Loane, George Guthrie, Peter Gurry, and Luke Wisely, along with our friends at St Andrews the Great.

I am grateful for the provision of leave granted to me by Stuart Coulton and the board of Sydney Missionary and Bible College. Without the generosity and support of the College this project would likely not have made it off the ground. Of special mention, Kit Barker and the Rev. Dr Sam Chan provided great sounding boards through the process of writing the book by providing theological insight, good coffee, and plenty of laughs. Bernie Cueto, Peter and Cornelia Tyrrell, David and Marsha Hammock, Murray Smith, and Jono Dykes were also terrific sources of encouragement. My former teaching assistant Greg Turner aided with research as did Mark North. I'm also thankful for the helpful contribution of Margaret Wilkins for her careful editing of this book, along with her helpful suggestions.

Stephen and Michelle Trew have been a constant source of encouragement over the last decade of ministry. Many of the ideas reflected in the book began with conversations with Stephen over breakfast in Sydney's CBD. Stephen's wisdom, humility, and interest in learning have stimulated me to reflect deeply over the images contained in this work. Michelle's special ministry of practical support and encouragement, particularly to Tamara and the kids, has been a significant blessing. We are deeply grateful to God for our friends the Trews.

My biggest thanks go to my lovely wife Tamara and our fabulous kids, Annabel, Adam, and Zara. Traveling around the world as a family of five for six months is no easy task. In spite of the challenges, however, everyone chimed in to make this a real adventure. Bicycle riding through the streets

Acknowledgments

of Cambridge, floating in the Dead Sea, feeding reindeer in the highlands of Scotland, and eating Dairy Queen in Texas, will be things we'll never forget. Finally, to Tamara I dedicate this book. You are a loving wife, a beautiful mother, a caring friend, and most importantly a faithful follower of the Lord Jesus. I'm privileged to be your partner in the pilgrimage to the celestial city. I hope for many more good years with you, my lady.

Abbreviations

BDAG   Walter Bauer, *A Greek-English Lexicon of the New Testament and Other Early Christian Literature*, ed. Frederick W. Danker, 3rd ed. (Chicago: University of Chicago Press, 2000).

BGU   *Aegyptische Urkunden aus den Koniglichen Staatlichen Museen zu Berlin Griechische Urkunden*, 15 vols. (Berlin, 1895–1983).

ESV   English Standard Version

LCL   Loeb Classical Library

NLT   New Living Translation

1

The Christian
What's in a Name?

> "The disciples were called Christians first at Antioch."
> —ACTS 11:26

POLYCARP OF SMYRNA WAS an old man when incarcerated by the Roman authorities. Hardly a rabble-rouser, the eighty-six-year-old Polycarp was in the twilight years of his life and by all accounts a peaceful and highly respectable man when mounted police and soldiers closed in on his small rural cottage to arrest him. Aware of his impending capture, Polycarp remained composed and simply prayed for God's will to be done. When the authorities finally arrived they were greeted not by a reluctant and adversarial criminal but by an aged man of grace who kindly beckoned them in. The document, *Martyrdom of Polycarp*, records:

> . . . when he [Polycarp] heard that they had arrived, he went and talked with them, while those who were present marveled at his age and his composure, and wondered why there was so much eagerness for the arrest of an old man like him. Then he immediately ordered that a table be set for them to eat and drink as much as they wished at that hour, and he asked them to grant him an hour so that he might pray undisturbed. When they consented, he stood and prayed, so full of the grace of God that for two hours he was

unable to stop speaking; those who heard him were amazed, and many regretted that they had come after such a godly old man.[1]

The soldiers arrested Polycarp and escorted him off to be tried by the proconsul. As he entered the stadium where he faced his trial the tumultuous crowd awaiting his appearance rose to their feet in one voice baying for his blood. Facing the raucous crowd the aged Polycarp looked around and paused when a voice from heaven was heard to say, "Be strong, Polycarp, and act like a man." Remaining composed Polycarp stood courageously before the proconsul and the trial began. "Swear by the Genius of Caesar," the proconsul demanded. To swear by the "Genius of Caesar" signified one's allegiance to the emperor, and this was something Polycarp could not bring himself to do. With firm resolve Polycarp stood silent and refused the demand. Again the proconsul pressed him, "Swear the oath, and I will release you; *revile Christ.*" With conviction in his voice, Polycarp responded, "For eighty-six years I have been his servant, and he has done me no wrong. How can I blaspheme my King who saved me?" He continued, "If you vainly suppose that I will swear by the Genius of Caesar, as you request, and pretend not to know who I am, listen carefully: *I am a Christian.*"[2]

For Polycarp, and for thousands in the centuries that have followed, identifying with Christ meant everything. As he stood on the precipice of death, Polycarp so valued the name of "Christian" that he would willingly choose execution over the betrayal of Christ. His identification with Jesus of Nazareth meant more to him than freedom and physical safety. Owning Christ was ultimate in the thinking and practice of Polycarp.

The difficult and costly decision of following Christ demonstrated by Polycarp is something that is mirrored everyday in the lives of "Christians" all over the world. While death is not always on the line, the cost of allegiance to Christ remains high for those who choose to be known as "Christian." It is the pastor in Asia who, as a result of being a "Christian," finds himself in a cold prison cell facing hardship and the very real possibility of death. It is the young man living in Indonesia where his confessing Christ has resulted in his inability to find a job. It is the Australian couple who, because they are "Christians," abandon their lucrative professions in order to care for street kids in Brazil. All over the world people sacrifice their comfort, careers, and relationships to demonstrate their allegiance to

---

1. *Martyrdom of Polycarp*, 7.2–3 (Holmes, trans.).
2. Ibid., 9.3–10.1.

Christ. But why do they make such extreme choices? The answer is bound up in the very title that they ascribe to themselves; namely, "Christians."

WHAT IS A "CHRISTIAN"?

I wonder what comes to your mind when you hear the word "Christian"? Were you to pose to the average person on the street what is meant by the name you would quickly gather there is considerable confusion over the term. For some the title of "Christian" is clearly negative. In the popular and long-lasting TV sitcom, *The Simpsons*, one of the minor characters of the show is Ned Flanders, who is presented as the archetype of a Christian. In the show Ned portrays the well meaning religious guy who attends church, tries to lives out his beliefs, and is generally a friendly and pretty moral person. Although he is characterized in this way, he is also presented as one who has a naïveté and a general ignorance of the world. A sincere person that, though likeable, is more interested in keeping rules than dealing with reality. For many people, Ned Flanders is a picture of the quintessential Christian. They perceive that being a Christian involves basically attending church, keeping rules, and trying to be a good person.

Others, however, understand the term "Christian" as an indicator of one's cultural heritage. When I was a boy at school, for example, we had a class called "Religious Education" where one of the options of self-classification was "Christian." At the start of the year the class teacher would ask each student to state his or her religious affiliation. Many of my friends who had no apparent connection to any church or any awareness of the teachings of Christianity would, nevertheless, classify themselves as "Christian." When asked why they would simply shrug their shoulders and say, "I was born in Australia so I guess I'm a Christian." This schoolyard assessment of religious faith is common even among many adults. For many, categories such as Christian, Jewish, Muslim are not so much related to beliefs and practices that they adhere to but indicators of one's cultural heritage or place of birth. Whereas some conclude that a Christian is simply a conservative rule-keeper, others assume that a Christian is someone from a particular cultural heritage. As one author explains:

> For some, being "Christian" is primarily cultural and traditional, a nominal title inherited from a previous generation, the net effect of which involves avoiding certain behaviors and occasionally attending church. For others, being a Christian is largely political,

a quest to defend moral values in the public square or perhaps to preserve those values by withdrawing from the public square altogether. Still more define Christianity in terms of a past religious experience, a general belief in Jesus, or a desire to be a good person.[3]

Clearly there is a general haze surrounding the commonly used term "Christian." In light of this, to best understand what a "Christian" is, we should probably begin with the title's origin.

THE TITLE "CHRISTIAN"

The term "Christian" finds its beginning in the Bible where it is found three times.

> So for a whole year Barnabas and Saul met with the church and taught great numbers of people. The disciples were called *Christians* first at Antioch. (Acts 11:26)
>
> Then Agrippa said to Paul, "Do you think that in such a short time you can persuade me to be a *Christian*?" (Acts 26:28)
>
> However, if you suffer as a *Christian*, do not be ashamed, but praise God that you bear that name. (1 Pet 4:16)

A few observations can be made about the title from these verses.

CHRISTIAN: THE NEED FOR A NAME

The first thing to be observed about the name "Christian" is the infrequency of the actual term. Although the term was used early in the history of the church, it was not the primary or initial branding of the movement that followed Jesus. Titles such as "disciple" and "followers of the way" were far more frequent than the title "Christian." As Acts 11:26 points out, the early followers of Jesus were most commonly referred to as "disciples." In Jewish culture it was not unusual to be the "disciple" of a rabbi or religious teacher. The early church perpetuated the Jewish practice and were simply "disciples" or "learners" who had attached themselves to the rabbi Jesus from Galilee.

---

3. MacArthur, *Slave*, 10.

The Christian

With the early church being predominantly Jewish there was no obvious need for the movement that accepted Jesus as the Messiah (Christ) to have its own unique title. The early church viewed its existence as an extension and indeed the continuation of the people of God from the Old Testament. The followers of Jesus believed that he was the fulfillment to the great promises of the Old Testament where God spoke of his Messiah who would rule on David's throne forever (2 Sam 7:8–16).

As the early church grew, however, it shifted from being a predominantly Jewish gathering to a collective that was largely non-Jewish, that is to say Gentile. Jesus had charged his disciples to take the gospel to "the ends of the earth" (Acts 1:8) and by the time of Acts 11 we find that the church was beginning to flourish outside of Jerusalem and Judea in places like Antioch. Although Antioch had a sizeable Jewish community it was largely non-Jewish in demographic. It was in this chiefly Gentile city that "the disciples were called *Christians* first" (Acts 11:26). Although their teaching was still firmly rooted to the Old Testament, and Jesus understood as the fulfillment of promise, the movement was now distinct enough in its cultural make-up and belief in Jesus as the Christ that the term "Christian" came into existence.

CHRISTIAN: THE SPREAD OF THE TERM

A second thing we observe about the term "Christian" is its element of popularity among those outside of the church. As the book of Acts concludes we find Paul taking the message of Jesus the Messiah to Rome, the very heart of the empire. In one of the events leading up to his Roman imprisonment we find the Apostle Paul on trial before the Herodian ruler Agrippa. As Paul faces prosecution he elucidates the foundation of his belief to Agrippa. The apostle explains that Jesus had come from God and was the great fulfillment of Old Testament hope. While addressing Agrippa, Paul declares, "I am saying nothing beyond what the prophets and Moses said would happen—that the Messiah would suffer and, as the first to rise from the dead, would bring the message of light to his own people and to the Gentiles" (Acts 26:22–23).

In addressing Agrippa the Apostle Paul articulates that at the very heart of his mission was the central belief that Jesus was the Christ. Paul clearly frames his personal identity as a follower or disciple of Jesus. In reply to Paul's assertion Agrippa asks the apostle, "Do you think in such a short time you can persuade me to be a *Christian*?" (Acts 26:28). Agrippa, the Herodian ruler, was noticeably aware that there was a movement of people known as "Christians." Paul does not refute Agrippa's use of the term, and indeed welcomes Agrippa's question with the response, "Short time or long—I pray that not only you but all who are listening to me today may become what I am, except for these chains" (Acts 26:29). The term "Christian" then was not simply a title utilized by a group in Antioch, but had reached the highest echelons of society.

CHRISTIAN: A TERM OF DERISION

The popularity of the term "Christian" flourished as the gospel message of Jesus spread throughout the empire. A few decades after the resurrection and ascension of Jesus, the Apostle Peter wrote the first of his letters while in Rome (1 Pet 5:13). Writing sometime during the Neronian persecution of the church in AD 64–68, Peter exhorted his readers, "if you suffer as a *Christian*, do not be ashamed, but praise God that you bear that name" (1 Pet 4:16).

A few things stand out about Peter's appeal. First, Peter is assuming that suffering "as a Christian" is a very real prospect. While it is possible to suffer for doing the wrong things, such as "criminal," "thief," or "meddler" (1 Pet 4:15), Peter has in mind suffering because of identifying with Jesus. Throughout 1 Peter the recurring theme is that of suffering as a follower of Christ. Peter anticipates those identifying with the Christ will naturally suffer in some form just as Jesus had.

Second, we also notice that there was the possibility of being "ashamed" of bearing the name "Christian." The background of the term "Christian" is interesting at this point. The word "Christian" is a Latinized form of the Greek word *Christos* which equates to the Hebrew idea of an "anointed one" or "messiah." Most likely the term was coined not by those in the church but by those outside of it. Concerning the origin of the title, the respected historian Edwin Judge comments:

> Like many others they [Christians] could be labeled conveniently from the god whose patronage they claimed. "Christ-ites" is certainly not the sort of name they would have chosen for themselves; but they seem to have had no agreed terminology, and most of the phrases they used, such as "sanctified" and "the brothers," were hardly likely to pass over into general usage when they merely

denoted in a vague way the kind of satisfaction offered by many other parallel societies. The Jews are the last persons who would have coined such a word as "Christian," which to them would have conceded the very point about the Messiahship of Jesus that they denounced as heretical; the followers of Jesus were simply "the sect of the Nazarenes." (Acts 24:5)[4]

The term "Christian" was simply the person-on-the-street vernacular for someone associated with the one who was called the "Christ." It was not intended as a compliment or a respected title but more likely a disapproving title of derision.

That the name "Christian" was something one may have been tempted to downplay can be seen in the writing of the Roman historian Tacitus. Tacitus recounts the persecution of the early Christians under Nero.

> [Nero] punished with the utmost refinements of cruelty, a class of men, loathed for their vices, whom the crowd styled *Christians*. *Christus*, the founder of the name had undergone the death penalty in the reign of Tiberius, by sentence of the procurator Pontius Pilate, and the pernicious superstition was checked for a moment, only to break out once more, not merely in Judaea, the home of the disease, but in the capital itself, where all things horrible or shameful in the world collect and find a vogue. First, then, the confessed members of the sect were arrested; next, on their disclosures, vast numbers were convicted, not so much on the count of arson as for hatred of the human race. And derision accompanied their end: they were covered with wild beasts' skins and torn to death by dogs; or they were fastened on crosses, and, when daylight failed, were burned to serve as lamps by night. Nero had offered his gardens for the spectacle, and gave an exhibition in his Circus, mixing with the crowd in the habit of a charioteer, or mounted in his car.[5]

From Tacitus's record we see that the followers of "Christus" were called "Christians" by "the crowd." Tacitus describes them as "a class of men loathed for their vices" and goes into great detail about how they were "punished." Clearly from these references we can see that identifying with Jesus and being known as a "Christian" was no light decision. Identification with Jesus was normally met with suspicion, disdain, and often persecution.

---

4. Judge, *Social Distinctives*, 31.
5. Tacitus, *Annals,* 15.44 (Jackson, trans.).

The contempt people had for the name "Christian" can still be felt today. In many parts of the world the message of Jesus is still considered foolishness as it was in the early days after Jesus' death and resurrection (cf. 1 Cor 1:18). Just as the early believers in Christ suffered, so also today there are a record number of people who are persecuted because of their identification with Christ. In countries all around the world to identify with Christ often results in the loss of job, the rejection of peers, and even the excommunication from one's family. Being a Christian means bearing his name, and this is no easy title to carry.

Recently I spoke at an event where I encountered a young man who had recently moved to Australia from a Middle Eastern country. This capable man had grown up his whole life practicing rituals like prayer, fasting, and giving, but he felt that God was unknowable and distant. Upon relocating to Australia he encountered a Christian student at university who befriended him and helped him learn English. Upon developing his friendship with the Christian student the young Middle Eastern man began to attend a Christian church with his friend. It was while attending a church that he heard, for the first time in his life, about God's love demonstrated through Jesus.

After a period of time had gone by the young man had become convinced that God was indeed knowable and had revealed himself in Jesus. In my conversation with this young man I explained the importance of trusting in Christ, and Christ alone, for the forgiveness of sin. At this point the young man became quite distressed. When I asked whether he wanted to receive Christ he indicated to me that owning the name of Christ was an enormous decision. "In my country," he explained, "converting to follow Christ means the death penalty. It will mean being rejected by my family. It will mean everything."

As I spoke with this man I wondered at how comfortable I had become with owning the name Christ. For many of us the name "Christian" is something that is fairly positive or at the least neutral in our cultural context. For others, however, the name "Christian" comes at a high price. Owning "Christ" invites derision and ridicule, and in some contexts even death.

CHRISTIAN: A BADGE OF HONOR

In spite of the very real danger of associating with Christ, Peter urged the first-century believers not to "be ashamed" but to "praise God" that they "bear that name" (1 Pet 4:16). For the outsider the term "Christian" was clearly uncomplimentary. For the believer, however, Peter says it is something to "praise God" for. Peter reveals the reason for praise when he explains, "If you are insulted because of the name of Christ, you are blessed, *for the Spirit of glory and of God rests on you*" (1 Pet 4:14). Suffering for the sake of God's reputation is to be expected in a world that rejects his lordship. Rejection on the basis of identification with Christ does not, however, go unnoticed by God. Jesus reminds his disciples that, "Blessed are you when people insult you, persecute you and falsely say all kinds of evil against you because of me. Rejoice and be glad, because great is your reward in heaven, for in the same way they persecuted the prophets who were before you" (Matt 5:11–12). For the one suffering for the name of Christ right now, the encouragement is to stay strong and follow the example of the Lord Jesus, knowing that his Spirit rests upon the one seeking his glory.

Owning the name of Christ in the midst of suffering hardship can be very difficult. Yet, for the follower of Jesus the name "Christian" represents the very heart of who we are. As the Christ suffered, so must we be prepared as we follow his steps. This truth is beautifully articulated in the poem *Hast Thou No Scar* by missionary Amy Carmichael. She wrote:

> Hast thou no scar?
> No hidden scar on foot, or side, or hand?
> I hear thee sung as mighty in the land,
> I hear them hail thy bright ascendant star,
> hast thou no scar?
>
> Hast thou no wound?
> Yet I was wounded by the archers, spent,
> leaned Me against a tree to die; and rent
> by ravening wolves that compassed me, I swooned:
> hast thou no wound?
>
> No wound? no scar?
> Yet, as the Master shall the servant be,
> and pierced are the feet that follow Me;

but thine are whole: can he have followed far
who hath no wound nor scar?[6]

These profound words of Amy Carmichael were not born from a woman living a comfortable life of ease but a hardworking missionary who spent fifty-six difficult years, including twenty bed-ridden years, ministering to the poor and destitute children of India. In her personal calamities Amy sought to make Christ known as her badge of honor and her delight. For Amy, suffering was not seen as a curse but an opportunity to mirror the Master.

To be a Christian carries the notion that, regardless of external circumstances, one will live to reflect the Lord Jesus. The very essence of being a Christian is to be committed to his lordship and demonstrating this by owning the name through following his example, reflecting his character, submitting to his teaching, and demonstrating his love.

SO WHAT?

In life we all tend to identify ourselves by something. For some of us, it is our cultural heritage, for others of us, our profession, still others of us define ourselves by our accomplishments or financial prosperity. For the people of God, however, primary identification comes not on the basis of our social standing in this world, but on the basis of who we are in relation to God. Our acceptance, security, and identity are found in the fact that we are accepted before God on the basis of our identity "in Christ." We are "God's handiwork, created in Christ Jesus to do good works" (Eph 2:10).

As "Christians" we are called to make Christ known, to live for his reputation and glory, and to introduce others to him. To be a "Christian" is to define your value not on accomplishments but in your identity as it relates to Christ. Though this will not always be easy, we are to "praise God" that we "bear that name."

So what does this look like?

1. Own the Name "Christian"

In most cultures of the world you will find that there is a general acceptance of someone believing in a great spiritual being or god(s). In light of this, to

---

6. Carmichael, *Gold Cord*, 10.

The Christian

verbalize a belief in "God" is culturally acceptable and fairly safe. When, however, one identifies with Christ Jesus, the Savior, not just an undefined belief in gods, things can become quite uncomfortable. To speak of God in generic terms is not necessarily wrong, but as we see in Scripture the practice of the early church was to proclaim specifically Jesus Christ. To know God one needed to know about Jesus Christ. Speaking about Jesus the Apostle Peter said, "Salvation is found in no one else, for there is no other name under heaven given to mankind by which we must be saved" (Acts 4:12).

When asked about our beliefs, the temptation is to converse *generically* about God. We need, however, to get into the habit of articulating more *specifically* who Jesus Christ is. Owning the name of Christ and identifying with him is central to who we are and what we are all about. We are *Christ-ians*. We need to cultivate the dangerous habit of mentioning Jesus' name in our conversations about spiritual things. It was the practice of the early church and it should be our practice as well.

2. Honor the Name "Christian"

In the Apostle Peter's day, as in ours, Christians often suffered for their association with Jesus. As Jesus suffered we too may now have to undergo hardship because of him. Rather than being ashamed, embarrassed, or concerned whether we will be liked or accepted by those around us, we must first and foremost be committed to honoring Jesus' reputation.

Over the last few years I have befriended a man named Jim. Jim grew up in a Christian home but he would not identify himself as a Christian. My mate Jim knows what I do for a living as I've talked about my job as a lecturer at a Bible college. I've spoken about things I teach such as Greek, the history of the New Testament, and preaching. Jim's interest in what I do has been piqued at different times and we have enjoyed our moments of dialogue over spiritual issues. Recently I noticed that Jim had become quite comfortable canvassing broad spiritual issues with me. As a result of this I decided to be more upfront in regard to what I believe. I shared with Jim how Jesus had made a difference in my life and I gently questioned Jim about his thoughts on the person of Jesus Christ. After an extended, awkward, and drawn-out silence, Jim quickly blurted out an ambiguous answer and hastily departed.

What I've noticed in discussions with people like Jim is that Jesus is always a central point of contention. It is far safer and easier not to mention Jesus in those sorts of exchanges. While there are friends and family who may not want to talk with us about Jesus, or find him too confronting, we must constantly, however, remind ourselves that he is our badge of honor and the cornerstone of our identity. I belong to Jesus and he is the one in whom I delight and serve. Jesus, more than my reputation or perceived self worth, is to be the center of my existence. I must keep making much of him, even if it means rejection, ridicule, or persecution from those around me.

3. Praise God for Bearing the Name "Christian"

The great narrative of the Bible culminates in the truth that "Jesus Christ is Lord" and in him alone is eternal life. The story of the Bible begins by revealing that our rebellion against God has resulted in death and isolation from him. The Old Testament is filled with stories of a common humanity that was broken, wrecked, and out of control. In spite of this, however, God in his mercy and grace spoke words of promise that he would bring restoration, newness, and redemption. He would fulfill these words of hope through his promised Messiah, the Christ. With the appearing of Jesus, this hope has now arrived and the promises fulfilled. Anyone of us can come to God by simply acknowledging our need for a Savior, accepting that Jesus is that Savior, and trusting that his work of dying and rising again is entirely sufficient to make us right with God. By receiving God's gracious gift of forgiveness and turning to Christ in contrition we can receive his mercy and live in security knowing that God accepts us "in Christ."

Knowledge of this wonderful forgiveness we have in Christ should compel us to praise him. Constantly reminding ourselves that we are accepted by God, not on the basis of our own achievements, but solely on our identification with Christ should lead us to deep relief, overflowing joy, and an assured peace. Whether we've known the good news of Jesus one day, or sixty years, the truth is still the same. It is because of this saving work we "praise God" who allows us to "bear that name."

Being a "Christian" is not something we deserve; indeed, we never live up to the title. In spite of this, however, God accepts us through Christ. So we are to praise him thankfully, purposefully, and frequently. We should praise him through song in the car with the kids. We should praise him in our hearts as we commute to work on the train. We should praise him publicly and in community as we share with others how good he is. We should make much of Christ because he graciously allows us to "bear that name" associated with him.

REFLECTIONS

1. Read 1 Peter 4:16. In what ways are we tempted to downplay owning the name of Christ? How does Peter exhort us to overcome this?
2. In conversations about our Christian faith we can often speak in generalities about God and avoid speaking directly about Jesus. What are some ways that you can bring about more intentional discussion about Jesus?
3. Finish this sentence, "God, I want to make Jesus Christ known in my context by . . .
4. Write out by name those in your context before whom you would like to bear the name of Christ. Pray about opportunities to share Jesus with them.

PRAYER

> Kind Father,
> Thank you that in your Son Jesus Christ I can now know you and stand forgiven before you. Forgive me for seeking to find my identity in other things such as my culture, my occupation, and my social standing. Help me to see past the fleeting popularity of the inadequate things of this world and assist me to build my life around my identity in Christ. Help me to bear the name "Christian" as I seek to praise you in all that I do and say. May people see in me the traits of your glorious Son Jesus in whose name I pray.
> Amen.

2

The Christian as Pilgrim

> Guide me, O Thou great Jehovah,
> Pilgrim through this barren land.
> I am weak, but Thou art mighty;
> Hold me with Thy powerful hand.
> Bread of Heaven, Bread of Heaven,
> Feed me till I want no more;
> Feed me till I want no more.
>
> —William Williams, 1745

> "All these people were still living by faith when they died. They did not receive the things promised; they only saw them and welcomed them from a distance, admitting that they were foreigners and strangers on earth."
>
> —Hebrews 11:13

Outside of the Bible, the book *The Pilgrim's Progress* has probably been the most influential and widely read Christian volume ever written. This work, penned during the 1600s, has been lauded by a variety of people throughout history including those identifying themselves as Christian and those not. Among others, the author Rudyard Kipling, the philosopher David Hume, and the famous British preacher Charles Spurgeon all had a deep fondness of the work. The book itself is an extraordinarily clever allegory of a man named "Christian" who makes a journey from the wilderness of the world to a celestial city. Few books in history have lasted more than one hundred years, yet *The Pilgrim's Progress* continues to be read and published well over three hundred years after its writing. What about this book makes it so timeless? What is it that makes this book so intriguing to both young and old? The answer, at least in part, lies in the background and context of its author, John Bunyan.

John Bunyan was an Englishman born in 1628. Growing up, John endured a difficult childhood. His family struggled financially as they sought their way forward in their insignificant rural community. As a sixteen year old John suffered what would be a string of personal tragedies in his life, beginning with both his mother and sister passing away within the same year. A distraught John wandered somewhat aimlessly through the next few years of his life. The troubled young man meandered into his twenties with little ambition and was known for very little, other than his vulgar use of the English language. At the age of twenty-one, however, John married and soon after this renounced his past wanderings and dedicated his life to following Christ.

The early days of his Christian life were not easy for John. When his first daughter Mary was born she was discovered to be blind. Living in a day and age where public health care was virtually non-existent, John and his wife did their best to care for their young daughter though it was very difficult. In the midst of his tumultuous circumstances, however, John continued to rely on Christ as he was utterly convinced that his God was benevolent and sovereign. In fact, though his struggles did not abate, John increasingly began to make known to others that Jesus Christ brought hope and good news to all who were downcast and needy. John's enthusiasm for the gospel message spilled over into his daily living and he started to openly preach of God's forgiveness to all who would listen.

Looking after his family consumed a lot of John's time and energy, as his family quickly grew to number four children. The unique challenges of raising a child with special needs, as well as providing for his growing family, was to take an even more challenging twist when his wife died suddenly, leaving him to raise four children by himself. Such circumstances, that would crush most of us, John handled with poise and courage. He bravely continued loving, serving, and providing for his family while at the time extensively preaching Christ in a variety of contexts. John's reputation as a preacher was spreading fast and it would not be too long before his obedience in spreading the gospel led to the most surprising of opposition: namely, the Church of England.

In John Bunyan's time the Church of England had a strict control on who could minister the word of God. A preacher, according to the Church of England, had to have their official sanction. Bunyan, however, felt no biblical conviction or moral obligation to be "licensed" by the state church. As a result John Bunyan had no hesitation about traveling and freely proclaiming the message of Jesus. After refusing to be quiet, at the request of the Church of England, John was incarcerated in 1660 in what would be the first of many imprisonments for preaching without the Church's permission.

It was during his multiple imprisonments that John Bunyan reflected more deeply on the Christian life. He wrote several small pieces about his struggle as a follower of Jesus. He loved to reflect on images like the "straight gate" and Jesus as "the light." The most well known of Bunyan's works, however, was when he reflected on the Christian as being like *a pilgrim* on a spiritual journey to a celestial city. The fruit of these reflections come to us now as the book, *The Pilgrim's Progress*.

What Bunyan was experiencing in his own life, he also saw reflected in the pages of Scripture where the Christian life, among other things, is painted as a pilgrimage or journey from one place to another. Bunyan studied the Bible and was drawn to the images of the Christian as a wanderer, a nomad, and a pilgrim. In this metaphor he grasped that the Christian life was not the way of ease and comfort; rather, it is represented as a difficult journey on which one meanders from one place to the next.

WHAT IS A PILGRIM?

The word "pilgrim" can convey a few different ideas. For some, the word represents someone undertaking a committed religious activity, normally involving travel to a destination. Many people, for example, travel to places like Jerusalem, Rome, or Mecca because of their religious convictions and refer to their travel as a spiritual "pilgrimage." For others, "pilgrim" is connected with the practice of exploration and journey. It does not have religious overtones, it is simply an individual or group traveling is search of a new home. This is the title often used, for example, of the early American settlers who are frequently referred to as "the Pilgrims."

Whatever the motivation, whether religious or otherwise, the term "pilgrim" implies the movement of a traveller journeying from one destination to another. This image is one consistently found in the Bible as it often uses language of travel, wandering, and journey throughout its pages. Frequently the language is used literally of people moving from destination to destination, but in other circumstances the imagery is used of a person or group on a spiritual journey. The theologian Alister McGrath picks up on this biblical theme commenting:

> The Bible is saturated with the image of a journey. Wherever we turn, we read of individuals making journeys. Perhaps the greatest of those was the forty-year journey of the people of Israel from their harsh captivity in Egypt to the Promised Land of Canaan. Elsewhere, we read of Abraham stepping out in faith to leave the land of his ancestors and go to a place chosen by God. He did not know where he was going, but he knew whom he would be traveling with, and that was good enough for him.
>
> We also read of pilgrims setting out to travel to Jerusalem, daunted by the thought of the mountains they must climb and the harsh conditions they will face, and yet consoled by the thought of the presence of God as they travel. We read of the people of Jerusalem returning home after their long period of exile in Babylon. The New Testament relates how the earliest term used to refer to Christians was "those who belong to the Way" (Acts 9:2).
>
> Thinking of the Christian life as a journey through the world offers us a vivid and helpful way of visualizing the life of faith . . . The image of a journey reminds us that we are *going somewhere* . . . Traveling does more than lead us to the goal of our journeying. A journey is itself a process that enables us to grow and develop as we press on to our goal.[1]

The Christian life is like a pilgrim on a journey from one destination to another. But where is the journey to and how is one to conduct oneself on the journey? To this we now turn our attention.

THE JOURNEY OF A PILGRIM

The Christian life, both in ancient times and today, has often been referred to as a *walk*. The popular cliché, for example, says that a Christian must "not only talk the talk but walk the walk." Used this way the term "walk"

---

1. McGrath, *The Journey*, 7–8.

is simply metaphoric language to talk about the way one *lives*. In the Old Testament we have dozens of references where "walking" is connected with living. For example,

> Blessed is the one who does not *walk* in step with the wicked. (Psalm 1:1)
> LORD, who may dwell in your sacred tent?
> Who may live on your holy mountain?
> The one whose *walk* is blameless,
> who does what is righteous,
> who speaks the truth from their heart. (Psalm 15:2)
>
> Whoever fears the LORD *walks* uprightly,
> but those who despise him are devious in their ways. (Prov 14:2)
>
> He has shown you, O mortal, what is good.
> And what does the LORD require of you?
> To act justly and to love mercy
> and to *walk* humbly with your God. (Mic 6:8)

Men like Enoch and Noah are described as people who were "walking faithfully" in the way they conducted their lives (Gen 5:22, 24; 6:9). In the Old Testament the image of walking pictures one journeying through life.

In the New Testament the term "walk" is used metaphorically thirty-nine times to represent the idea of *living*. As seen in the following examples, the "walking" language of the New Testament carries with it the same idea as the Old Testament use where the term represents how one lives.

> We *walk* by faith and not by sight. (2 Cor 5:7)
>
> So I say, *walk* by the Spirit. (Gal 5:16)
>
> If we claim to have fellowship with him yet *walk* in the darkness, we lie and do not live by the truth. But if we *walk* in the light, as he is in the light, we have fellowship with one another, and the blood of Jesus, his Son, purifies us from all sin. (1 John 1:6)
>
> Whoever claims to live in him must *walk* as Jesus did. (1 John 2:6)

The journey of the Christian life begins with recognition of Jesus' authority. In the gospels Jesus calls his disciples to "follow me" (Matt 9:9). While there was a literal call to walk with him, it is clear from his teaching elsewhere that Jesus' invitation was to accompany him on a spiritual journey. Being a disciple and walking after Jesus was not an easy task, as seen in his warning that, "whoever does not carry their cross and follow me cannot be my disciple" (Luke 14:27). Elsewhere Jesus leaves us with no doubt as to the journey's harshness when he says, "Foxes have dens and birds have nests, but the Son of Man has no place to lay his head" (Matt 8:20). Following Jesus on the journey entails times of difficulty and challenge, as demonstrated in his life, the lives of his disciples, John Bunyan, and scores of other pilgrims through church history.

The author of the book of Hebrews probably best encapsulates how we are to think of ourselves as pilgrims. The main theme of the book of Hebrews addresses the spiritual drift of those who were becoming distracted and discouraged by persecution as they followed after Christ on their journey. To encourage them to continue in their spiritual pilgrimage the author exhorts his readers to follow the Old Testament heroes of faith who had walked the journey before them. In Hebrew 11:8–12 the author presents Abraham as an example of a pilgrim *par excellence* who faithfully walked the journey with God. The author writes:

> By faith Abraham, when called to go to a place he would later receive as his inheritance, obeyed and went, even though he did not know where he was going. By faith he made his home in the promised land like a stranger in a foreign country; he lived in tents, as did Isaac and Jacob, who were heirs with him of the same promise. For he was looking forward to the city with foundations, whose architect and builder is God. And by faith even Sarah, who was past childbearing age, was enabled to bear children because she considered him faithful who had made the promise. And so from this one man, and he as good as dead, came descendants as numerous as the stars in the sky and as countless as the sand on the seashore.

From the life of Abraham there are three useful observations we can make about pilgrimage. The pilgrim (1) lives by faith, (2) lives as a stranger in the world, and (3) longs for their final destination.

The Pilgrim Lives by Faith

I first heard about the biblical character Abraham as a small child in a Sunday School class. We sang a song about him. The song? You guessed it, "Father Abraham had many sons, many sons had father Abraham." I would nod my head, shake my leg, turn around, sit down, and have the refrain stuck in my head for the rest of the day. What I didn't understand at the time was that this man Abraham of whom I was singing was probably the most significant figure in the entire Old Testament.

The story of Abraham is utterly surprising. We are first introduced to Abraham, or "Abram" as he was initially known, in Genesis 11. From this opening account we discover that Abram lived his early days with his extended family in the metropolitan "Ur of the Chaldeans" (Gen 11:31). A city man, Abram received a supernatural summons from God who then instructs him to depart his familiar surroundings in search of a different country, one that was at the time completely unknown to him.

> The Lord said to Abram, "Go from your country, your people and your father's household to the land I will show you. I will make you into a great nation, and I will bless you; I will make your name great, and you will be a blessing. I will bless those who bless you, and whoever curses you I will curse; and all the peoples on earth will be blessed through you." (Gen 12:1–3)

What is so striking about this whole scenario is that Abram, aged seventy-five, along with his elderly wife, takes God at his word and, though he has no idea on *how* God will accomplish the task, he believes in *faith* that God will accomplish it. Genesis 12:4 records the response to God's calling when it says, "so *Abram went* as the Lord told him."

Abraham's faith is simply astonishing. The author of Hebrews clarifies what was involved in his decision to travel as a pilgrim when the author records, "By faith Abraham, when called to go to a place he would later receive as his inheritance, obeyed and went, *even though he did not know where he was going*" (Heb 11:8). What a crazy step of faith! Can you imagine the conversation between Abraham and his wife?

> "Listen, Sarah, God has called me to leave to another country."
> "What?! Whereabouts, Abraham?"
> "I don't know exactly, but get the gear together, we're leaving."
> "How long will it take to get there?"
> "No idea. It will take as long as God intends the journey to be."
> "How do you know this is true, Abraham?"
> "God told me. By the way Sarah, we are going to have some children."

Abraham, in simple yet profound faith, takes God at his word and actively responds in light of that belief. He is unshakeable in his confidence

The Christian as Pilgrim

that God's word is true and reliable. He doesn't necessarily see the end goal at his calling, but he "obeyed and went." As a pilgrim, a traveler, someone on a journey, he trusts that God knows best, and that God will take him where he needs to go.

Living by faith is often extremely tough. When God bids us to follow his directions it can sometimes feel counterintuitive. From an external perspective it might even appear illogical or foolish. An example of this can be seen in the life of the missionary Charles (C. T.) Studd. Studd grew up in a wealthy family in Northamptonshire, England. C. T. and his brothers had many privileges, one of which was being educated at the renowned Eton College. After graduating from Eton, C. T. went on for further study at Trinity College in Cambridge. During his time in Cambridge C. T. began to excel at cricket culminating in his selection for the national team. In many ways C. T. Studd had the world at his feet. He had wealth, outstanding academic credentials, and he was fast becoming a national sporting star. Yet it was at this point C. T., like Abraham, made a decision of faith that was extremely radical. Upon graduating from Trinity College he felt compelled that God was calling him to serve as a missionary in China. With a successful career, social importance, and obvious luxuries beckoning him, C. T. Studd purposely relinquished his inheritance, packed his belongings, and left for the mission field where he would ultimately die.

Like Abraham, C. T. Studd trusted that God's plans and purposes were more valuable and enduring than his own. Studd lived with the firm belief that God's word and his promises were trustworthy and ultimate. Like Abraham, Studd saw his life as a journey of which God should lead. He forsook all that he saw as temporary and transient in order to follow Christ, whatever that looked like. C. T. Studd's faith and purpose can be seen in a poem attributed to him, entitled *Only One Life*.

> Two little lines I heard one day,
> Traveling along life's busy way;
> Bringing conviction to my heart,
> And from my mind would not depart;
> Only one life, 'twill soon be past,
> Only what's done for Christ will last.
>
> Only one life, the still small voice,
> Gently pleads for a better choice;
> Bidding me selfish aims to leave,

And to God's holy will to cleave;
Only one life, 'twill soon be past,
Only what's done for Christ will last.

Only one life, a few brief years,
Each with its burdens, hopes, and fears;
Each with its days I must fulfil,
living for self or in His will;
Only one life, 'twill soon be past,
Only what's done for Christ will last.

Give me, Father, a purpose deep,
In joy or sorrow Thy word to keep;
Faithful and true what e'er the strife,
Pleasing Thee in my daily life;
Only one life, 'twill soon be past,
Only what's done for Christ will last.

Only one life, yes only one,
Now let me say, "Thy will be done;"
And when at last I'll hear the call,
I know I'll say 'twas worth it all.
Only one life, 'twill soon be past,
Only what's done for Christ will last.[2]

Abraham and C. T. Studd both understood the importance of living by faith. They understood that "without faith it is impossible to please God" (Heb 11:6) so they intentioned to *"walk* by faith and not by sight" (2 Cor 5:7). The pilgrim may not always know where they are going, but if by faith they are trusting God's leading and his promises then they will ultimately succeed in finding their purpose and God's peace.

The Pilgrim Lives as a Stranger

The second thing to notice about Abraham's pilgrimage was that he abandoned the security of his home environment to live as an outsider in an

---

2. The publication of the poem is unknown and was likely part of one of the many tracts C. T. Studd published. For a short account of Studd's life see Pollock, *The Cambridge Seven*.

unknown country. The author of Hebrews explains, "By faith he made his home in the promised land like *a stranger* in a foreign country; he lived in tents, as did Isaac and Jacob, who were heirs with him of the same promise" (11:9). Abraham lived in a context that was unfamiliar, different, and probably culturally distant. He made Canaan his home, but it was not his natural home.

In a small measure, I'm familiar with what it is like to live as a stranger in a foreign country. Over the course of my life I have travelled to forty countries but have lived extended periods in three countries. My first international move occurred when I was fourteen years old and it was decided that we, as a family, would move from Australia to New Zealand. Most would think leaving a small rural Australian town would be an exciting venture, but to be honest I was filled with dread. In our little town I knew everybody, was settled at school, and generally fit in. Moving away from the comfort of the known to the relatively unknown filled me with considerable angst.

As expected, the move from one country to another resulted in significant changes. Relocating from rural, white, middle-class Australia to the largest Polynesian city in the world, the city of Auckland, was a pleasant change but a cultural change nonetheless. I went from being the normal, accepted, stock standard country kid to being atypical. I looked, felt, and spoke differently than those around me. While I was a resident of New Zealand, I was a stranger, a foreigner, and an outsider much like Abraham.

A pilgrim by nature is a traveler on a journey who will often seem different. A wayfarer may stop at a destination, even for an extended stay, but this does not mean that they will always fit in with those around them. I stood out in New Zealand for I was an Australian. Abraham stood out in Canaan, for this was not his natural homeland. In a similar vein, as Christians we live as those who, like the pilgrim of John Bunyan's story, are moving to the celestial city. We should, if we are living by faith, look, sound, speak, and act differently than those around us. In a very real sense we should *not* fit in with the world in which we live. Other writers in the New Testament pick up on this idea. Peter, for example, refers to the Christian believers as "*exiles* scattered throughout the provinces of Pontus, Galatia, Cappadocia, Asia and Bithynia" (1 Pet 1:1). James describes the Christian community as those "*scattered* among the nations" (Jam 1:1).

The Christian who understands their identity as a pilgrim will recognize that they are inherently different than those around them. They will, at times, feel that they don't belong in their context. The metaphor of the Christian as pilgrim is a reminder that our current abode is not the final destination. This can be seen in the description of Abraham's dwelling. Rather than settling down into retirement in a nice stone house with rolling hills and a sea view, Abraham and his sons "lived in tents" (Heb 11:9). As pilgrims they lived their journey with an eye on another destination. This brings us to a third observation regarding our pilgrimage, namely, our final destination.

The Pilgrim Longs for Their Final Destination

The pilgrim is on a journey to somewhere. They are making their way from point A to point B. This can be observed in the faithful pilgrimage of Abraham. God called Abraham to leave one place, Ur of the Chaldeans, and to go to another place (Gen 12:1–3). While we are left thinking that Canaan is the ultimate destination for Abraham, the author of Hebrews gives us further insight into the destination when he explains why Abraham and his sons "lived in tents" (11:9). In Heb 11:10 he explains that "he [Abraham] was looking forward to the city with foundations, whose architect and builder is God." Abraham's journey was not simply to the physical location of Canaan, but something so much more. Abraham's longing was for a city where God himself was. It is this forward-looking hope that the author of Hebrews wants his readers to imitate. The Christian life is not an aimless wandering about; rather, it is a life of faith and focus on the things yet to take place.

The New Testament speaks often of the believer's final destination. 1 Corinthians 15, for example, speaks of a great resurrection where God will completely and fully raise to life all of those "in Christ." On that great day God will be "all in all" (1 Cor 15:28). God's kingdom will come, all things will be made new, and his people will relish his presence for all eternity. Unfortunately, however, this is not yet a full reality as we live with the tension that we are between the first and the second comings of Christ. Though with Jesus' first appearing the old world has begun to pass away, we still long for the day when Christ returns and his kingdom comes in all of its fullness.

The author C.S. Lewis creatively picks up on this notion of hope in his book, *The Lion, the Witch, and the Wardrobe*. In the book he tells of four young travelers who, like pilgrims, are on a journey. In their journey we find a scene where they are wandering from a kingdom of fog and winter to a new kingdom where it is spring and there is wonderful life. We read:

> Every moment the patches of green grew bigger and the patches of snow grew smaller. Every moment more and more of the trees shook off their robes of snow. Soon, wherever you looked, instead of white shapes you saw the dark green of firs or the black prickly branches of bare oaks and beeches and elms. Then the mist turned from white to gold and presently cleared away altogether. Shafts of delicious sunlight struck down on to the forest floor and overhead you could see a blue sky between the treetops. Soon there were more wonderful things happening. Coming around a corner into a glade of silver birch trees Edmund saw the ground covered in all directions with little yellow flowers. The noise of the water grew louder. Presently they actually crossed a stream. Beyond it they found snowdrops growing... Then came a sound even more delicious than the sound of the water. Close beside the path they were following a bird suddenly chirped from the branch of a tree. It was answered by the chuckle of another bird a little further off. And then, as if that had been a signal, there was chattering and chirruping in every direction, and then a moment of full song, and within five minutes the whole wood was ringing with birds' music... There was no trace of fog now. The sky became bluer and bluer, and now there were white clouds hurrying across it from time to time... a light breeze sprang up... the trees began to come fully alive... a bee buzzed across their path. "This is no thaw," said the dwarf, suddenly stopping. "This is *Spring*. What are we to do? Your winter has been destroyed I tell you! This is Aslan's doing."[3]

This scene beautifully encapsulates what is true of our own experience. Though our destination is filled with life, joy, hope, and vibrancy, we are still moving through a kingdom that feels like a foggy English winter. The good news message of the gospel, however, is that because of the resurrection of Jesus spring has sprung. We are now to push beyond our wintery surrounds as we move to the light of the kingdom that is yet to be.

As pilgrims we long for the day, just as Abraham did, when we will dwell in the city of our great God. As we struggle with the humdrum of the journey, the metaphor of the pilgrim reminds us to keep our eyes on the destination. What will that destination be like? It will be a kingdom where God himself will abide.

3. Lewis, *The Lion, the Witch, and the Wardrobe*, 110–112.

Knowing Who You Are

> Now the dwelling of God is with men, and he will live with them. They will be his people, and God himself will be with them and be their God. (Rev 21:3)

Our destination is a perfect and new creation.

> All creation anticipates the day when it will join God's children in glorious freedom from death and decay. (Rom 8:21, NLT)

Our destination is an environment free of pain and suffering.

> He will remove all of their sorrows, and there will be no more death or sorrow or crying or pain. (Rev 21:4)

Our destination is a place where all longings are met.

> To all who are thirsty I will give the springs of the water of life, without charge! (Rev 21:6)

Our destination is a place of perfect intimacy with God.

> No longer will there be any curse. The throne of God and of the Lamb will be in the city, and his servants will serve him. They will see his face, and his name will be on their foreheads. (Rev 22:3–4)

As pilgrims we must remind ourselves that we are on a journey. Just as Abraham longed for his final destination so we also should yearn and groan with creation "for the children of God to be revealed" (Rom 8:19). Indeed, this yearning for a better home has always been the identifying mark of the children of God. Reflecting on the great heroes of faith the author of Hebrews concludes:

> All these people were still living by faith when they died. They did not receive the things promised; they only saw them and welcomed them from a distance, admitting that they were foreigners and strangers on earth. People who say such things show that they are looking for a country of their own. If they had been thinking of the country they had left, they would have had opportunity to return. Instead, they were longing for a better country—a heavenly one. Therefore God is not ashamed to be called their God, for he has prepared a city for them. (Heb 11:13–16)

The Christian as Pilgrim

The reality is that, like Abraham, we may never see the fullness of the kingdom in our current experience; yet, like Abraham, we sojourn in faith knowing that God's kingdom will come when Jesus returns in glory.

WHAT CAN WE LEARN FROM THE PILGRIM?

The New Testament, picking up from the Old Testament, regularly uses the image of pilgrimage as a metaphor for life. The Scriptures, as we've observed, remind us that as followers of Jesus we need to view ourselves as people on a journey. While we stumble along the path of life we are to keep our eyes firmly fixed on our future glory with Christ when his kingdom comes. With this in mind Paul, using the image of the pilgrim, urges us to "*walk* in a manner worthy of the calling to which you have been called" (Eph 4:1, ESV). But how do we do this?

1. As a Pilgrim Remember the Journey Is One of Faith

Following Christ is often countercultural and counterintuitive. When Christ authoritatively calls us to follow him he often leads us in directions we never thought of going. There are moments in our experience where we know that following Christ means making difficult decisions and choosing the road less traveled. It is the Christian businessman who turns down a promotion in order to better serve people in his local church. It is the Christian university student who, in obedience to Christ, would rather stay sexually pure than to follow the lead of promiscuity by those around them. It is the young couple who sacrifices promising professional careers in order to train for Bible translation in a developing country. Faith requires stepping out of our comfort zone and trusting God's word and leading. Faith requires costly obedience and almost always involves a measure of uncertainty.

As a young Christian this became very clear to me when I decided to go to Bible college. I entered college not really having any clear direction as to my future, other than wanting to know Christ more. I had no grand visions of "vocational ministry" and simply wanted to grow and help others to mature in Christ. As I journeyed through college I made the most of my education and relished the chance to learn. At the end of my studies, however, I was confronted with the commonly asked question, "What are you going to do next?" Inevitably this caused a bit of angst because I really didn't know! Through circumstances I felt led to continue my education and made my way to seminary and then later vocational Christian ministry.

If you had asked me as a first-year Bible college student where I would be in twenty years, I honestly couldn't have told you. Living by faith is a bit like that. The Bible says that God's word is "a lamp for my feet, a light on my path" (Psalm 119:11). In the ancient world one would use a "lamp" while traveling at night. With a lamp you could only see the next few paces in front of your feet. With a lamp you didn't see the whole street. If the whole street were lit you wouldn't need a lamp. God does not clearly map out before us all the details of our lives. Why? He does this because he wants us to walk by faith. He wants us to journey to our heavenly destination by faith as we depend upon his wisdom. The pilgrim on the way to what Bunyan called the "celestial city" must walk the journey trusting God to direct their steps. This will look different for all of us, but will *always* involve dependent obedience.

2. As a Pilgrim Remember the Journey Is Not Easy

Undoubtedly one of the reasons that *The Pilgrim's Progress* has been popular across different generations has been because those of us who have read it resonate with the struggles, lamentations, and pitfalls of the chief character, Christian. The Christian journey is often complicated to navigate. Jesus warned his followers, "in this world you will have trouble" (John 16:33). Paul was familiar with "troubles, hardships and distresses" (2 Cor 6:4). Though the believer's destination is fixed, walking the path of faith is anything but smooth.

As you and I journey toward our heavenly dwelling we must always keep in mind that the world as we see it now is not our ultimate destination. While we know this is true, many of us stop along the journey and settle into life as if the seventy years of our life is our ultimate destination. We view the purchase of a bigger home, a newer car, and a better computer as something that will make our journey complete. As C. S. Lewis explains, "We are half-hearted creatures, fooling around with drink and sex and ambition when infinite joy is offered us, like an ignorant child who wants to go on making mud pies in a slum because he cannot imagine what is meant by the offer of a holiday at the sea. We are far too easily pleased."[4]

---

4. Lewis, *The Weight of Glory*, 2.

The gospel calls us to follow Christ with full abandon but in order to gain our life we must be willing to lose it. Sadly, many of us start the journey but become all "too easily pleased" with the things along the way. Discipleship is not about temporary comfort but costly obedience, even in tough times.

3. As a Pilgrim Remember Your Final Destination Is Certain

Every year I spend quite a bit of time on planes. Periodically I will be required to take a long international flight. During these longer flights I constantly look for ways to keep myself entertained while on board. While many enjoy watching movies, playing games, listening to music, I am one of those quirky people who enjoy watching the flight maps on the inflight entertainment. I am happy to sit for hours, much to the amazement of those around me, watching the plane move inch by inch to the final destination. There is something comforting for me in counting down the hours, the miles, the cities, until our destination is reached.

Knowing where you are going on a journey is important. For the follower of Christ, the endpoint of the resurrected people of God is a redeemed creation where God rules and reigns. As pilgrims heading in this trajectory we must consistently remind ourselves that this is where we are going. Though the journey is long, it will be worth it. When we receive the phone call about the death of a loved one, we need to remember our destination. When that unexpected diagnosis is given, we need to recall where we are heading. When we're tempted to feel envious of our neighbor's new car, or recent holiday, we need to remind ourselves of our future eternal dwelling. We need to exhort our soul with the reality that there is "only one life, 'twill soon be past, only what's done for Christ will last."

As God's people, like John Bunyan's character "Christian," we are pilgrims on our way to a celestial city. So let us keep in mind the untarnished joys of heaven as we faithfully plod through our current journey. Let us echo in our hearts the hope that the imprisoned preacher John Bunyan had when he prayed, "O! who is able to conceive the inexpressible, inconceivable joys that are there? None but they who have tasted of them. Lord, help us to put such a value upon them here, that in order to prepare ourselves for them, we may be willing to forego the loss of all those deluding pleasures here."[5] Amen, and amen.

---

5. Bunyan, *The Complete Works of John Bunyan*, 81.

REFLECTIONS

1. What stands out to you about the Christian being like a *pilgrim*? What in this image is either new to you, or a helpful reminder? Share this with someone.

2. In life we can often become distracted on our journey. What objects tempt you to forget your final destination?

3. In this chapter the reminder has been to keep the final destination in mind as you journey through life. What is compelling about Christian hope? What is it about the coming kingdom of God that you actually yearn for?

4. Write down three concrete ways in which you can maintain a heavenward focus as you journey toward the celestial city.

PRAYER

Benevolent Lord,

Thank you that out of darkness you have called me into the light and life of your beloved Son the Lord Jesus Christ. As I follow him in my journey help me to remain thoroughly dependent upon the Holy Spirit to guide, sustain, and direct me. Keep me from being distracted by the weak desires of the world. Strengthen my focus on your coming kingdom as I live by faith and trust in your promises. Forgive me for my lack of desire for righteousness. Renew within me a deep and growing passion to see your name honored throughout the world. In the valleys of doubt and temptation, give me eyes to see, hands to serve, and feet to obey as I continue my pilgrimage.

Amen.

3

The Christian as Citizen

> "I am not an Athenian or a Greek, but a citizen of the world."
> —SOCRATES

> "But our citizenship is in heaven. And we eagerly await a Savior from there, the Lord Jesus Christ."
> —PHILIPPIANS 3:20

> "Incomparably more glorious than Rome, is that heavenly city in which for victory you have truth; for dignity, holiness; for peace, felicity; for life, eternity."
> —ST AUGUSTINE, CITY OF GOD

WHERE ARE YOU FROM? This is a simple enough question that I've been asked multiple times in my life. Unfortunately for me, however, I don't really have a concise answer. From a purely historic perspective, I could respond to the question with, "I'm was born in Newcastle, Australia." Though I my early years were spent in that great town, however, I don't really find my identity as someone from Newcastle as I haven't lived within that vicinity in decades. From a purely geographic perspective, I could reply by saying, "I'm a Sydney-sider." This would indicate that I currently identify myself with my place of residence in the cosmopolitan city of Sydney, Australia. While I love my city, however, the title itself does not really communicate who I am, or really where I am from. This is particularly true given I have lived in many cities. I have resided in Auckland, but I'm not an Aucklander. I have lived in Chicago, but I'm not a Chicagoan. I stayed seven years in Texas, but I am not a Texan. So where am I from?

If I were to step back and see the larger picture of my ancestors, the question of where I am from only grows more complicated. You see while my father is Australian, my mother is from New Zealand. So am I Australian or a New Zealander? This is complex. It is even more complicated when I reflect on the fact that my maternal grandfather migrated from Newton Mearns in Scotland and married an Australian whom he met in New Zealand. So am I a Novocastrian, a Sydney-sider, an Aussie, a New Zealander, or even a Scot? I'm just not sure. This issue of origin and identity will be even more complicated for my children given my wife is an Ecuadorian of indigenous and Italian background!

The issue of who we are is no small thing. In life we often search for meaning and identity. Sometimes we perceive that our core identity is bound up in what we do. We say, for example, "I am a pharmacist," "I am a printer," "I am a lawyer," or "I am a school teacher." Many of us when asked about ourselves default to describing the things that keep us occupied rather than our core beliefs, moral convictions, or family of origin. In some cultures this appears to be *the* key value in defining one's worth and significance. A successful career, a university degree, a title before or after one's name are seen to be the crucial indicators of one's worth.

At other times we highlight our identity on the basis of our relationships. "I am married to . . . " "I am the brother of . . . " "My father is . . . " In my family I have three siblings: Debbie, Deidre, and Dallas. So naturally with a name like Malcolm I feel the odd one out! Growing up with older siblings I found that a constant reply was made when I introduced myself: "Are you the brother of . . . ?" My identity was immediately connected to my family of origin. Indeed, familial relationships and who our forebears were matter to many of us. While I was living in America, for example, I was often amazed at how many people claimed they had ancestors who came to America on the Mayflower, and how many Chicagoans were Irish, particularly on St Patrick's Day! Many of us define ourselves not by what we do but on the basis of our cultural heritage and from which tribe we belong.

There are still others among us who find their identity enmeshed in the social networks that we participate in. For some of us, the advancement of social media such as Facebook, Instagram, and Twitter has allowed us to define ourselves through cyberspace. We interpret our significance on the mercurial basis of how many followers or friends respond to our posts or tweets. Others of us socially connect via more traditional means such as being members of clubs, lodges, associations, and charities. We gauge our status from the number of boards we are on, the number of client lunches we have, or even the number of meetings we are invited to.

While there is nothing inherently wrong with the search for identity, the Bible reveals that the center of our identity lies *not* primarily in what we do, who we are related to, or how popular we may or may not be. The Bible presents our value, our significance, and our identity in direct connection with our relationship to God. There is nothing wrong with being a banker, a preacher, or a kitchen hand, but our occupations are not the center of who we are. We were not created by God simply to define ourselves by our ancestral lineage or what ethnicity or tribe we have originated from. We do not exist to appraise our worth on how many people we connect with or how many people like us. You and I have been created in God's image to find our core identity in relationship to him.

The Bible clarifies the parameters of our connection to God with several images. We are, for example, likened to members of his body and children in his family, as well as being his servants. One image that is particularly helpful in defining our cultural identity, however, is to understand ourselves in light of the biblical metaphor of *citizenship*. The Scriptures identify our "citizenship" as being "in heaven" (Phil 3:20) and with "God's people" (Eph 2:19). Our loyalty and core affiliation are not to ourselves, our country of origin, or with the kingdom of this world, but they are with "the kingdom of our Lord, and of his Messiah" (Rev 11:15). In light of this, it would be helpful to consider the language and role of citizenship in the ancient world and then think through how that shapes the image presented in the Bible and its implications for us.

CITIZENSHIP IN THE ANCIENT WORLD

In the ancient world citizenship played a prominent role in cultural identification. Citizenship, depending upon which type, provided a means of membership into the cultural decision-making and leadership of the community. It could offer benefits of travel, legal protection, and aid in business dealings, and would give one a governing voice in society. A lack of citizenship, on the other hand, put one at considerable social disadvantage as certain rights and privileges would be denied.

Attaining citizenship was certainly not an easy task. In Athens, for example, to be accepted as a citizen required that both of your birth parents were freeborn Athenians.[1] If you had a father from Athens, but your mother was from another place such as Corinth, or Ephesus, or Macedonia, then you would be excluded from the Athenian register of citizens and subsequently not entitled to Athenian privileges. In Tarsus, where Paul was from, one needed not only to have the correct parentage but also equity of land worth five hundred drachmae.[2] Citizenship was normally acquired through birth (Acts 22:28), though it also could be purchased (Acts 22:28), or bestowed by the Empire itself.[3] Citizenship was certainly not the privilege of all people.

During the New Testament era there were different types of citizenships. One could be a citizen of a city like "Tarsus" (Acts 21:3), or a country like "Israel" (Eph 2:12). The most significant and recognized type of citizenship, however, was Roman citizenship. Renowned New Testament scholar F. F. Bruce observes the importance of Roman citizenship when writing about Paul's Tarsian citizenship:

> Paul was obviously proud of his status as a citizen of Tarsus, "no mean city" (Acts 21:39). He was evidently born into a family which possessed the citizenship . . . Paul's Tarsian citizenship, however, was not nearly so important in the world of his day as his Roman citizenship by birth, i.e., by inheritance from his father (Acts 22:28). Roman citizenship, originally restricted to the city of Rome, was prudently extended to select non-Romans as an honor for services rendered to Roman interests. The possession of Roman citizenship was a high social distinction in the Near East. Once conferred, it remained in the family.[4]

Clearly being a Roman citizen was a highly valuable commodity. Of the fifty million inhabitants of the Empire, only around five million enjoyed the status of being a free and full Roman citizen.[5] So while some, like the Apostle Paul, enjoyed the freedom and privileges of being a citizen of the Empire, others, like Jesus, did not have the same rights. Those, like Paul,

1. Aristotle, *Athenian Constitution*, 26.
2. Dio Chrysostom, *Discourses*, 34.23.
3. Josephus, for example, was granted Roman citizenship for his contribution to the Empire.
4. Bruce, "Citizenship," 1:1048.
5. Jeffers, *The Greco-Roman World*, 197.

who had Roman citizenship enjoyed a wide range of legal and practical benefits. One writer comments:

> The Roman citizen was privileged. Citizenship carried with it the right to hold political office and responsibility in the Roman state. It gave the right to participate in the deliberations of Roman assemblies. It gave the right to inherit Roman property and the right to contract a marriage under Roman law, with all its attendant rights and duties. More importantly, in day-to-day life it gave access to the Roman law, especially in regard to commerce and property . . . In theory the Roman citizen could travel anywhere without problems, being protected by the Roman law . . . He owed allegiance to Rome, and Rome would protect him.[6]

The book of Acts records several occasions when the Apostle Paul made the most of his privileged Roman citizenship. First, it no doubt gifted him with the freedom to travel unhindered and provided the perfect platform to preach about Jesus in every corner of the known Empire. Second, we discover several times where Paul used his Roman citizenship in an effort to be accorded due legal process. In Acts 22:22–29, for example, Paul when tried before a crowd in Jerusalem utilized his Roman citizenship for his protection.

> The crowd listened to Paul until he said this. Then they raised their voices and shouted, "Rid the earth of him! He's not fit to live!" As they were shouting and throwing off their cloaks and flinging dust into the air, the commander ordered that Paul be taken into the barracks. He directed that he be flogged and interrogated in order to find out why the people were shouting at him like this. As they stretched him out to flog him, Paul said to the centurion standing there, "Is it legal for you to flog a *Roman citizen* who hasn't even been found guilty?" When the centurion heard this, he went to the commander and reported it. "What are you going to do?" he asked. "This man is a Roman citizen." The commander went to Paul and asked, "Tell me, are you a Roman citizen?" "Yes, I am," he answered. Then the commander said, "I had to pay a lot of money for my citizenship." "But I was born a citizen," Paul replied. Those who were about to interrogate him withdrew immediately. The commander himself was alarmed when he realized that he had put Paul, *a Roman citizen*, in chains.

---

6. Lyall, *Slaves, Citizens, Sons*, 61–62.

The Apostle Paul employed his Roman citizenship at the appropriate time in order to facilitate a fair trial and ultimately to leverage further opportunity for him to freely preach the gospel.[7] Citizenship of Rome was not a negative thing for Paul, but provided a helpful platform for him to further the work of Christ.

THE TENSION OF DUAL CITIZENSHIP

Allegiance to Rome and its leader was significant in the first century. To honor and to demonstrate loyalty to the emperor was the responsibility of every person whether citizen or not, with no exception. With the arrival of Jesus, however, the Christian community faced a genuine dilemma. While they were, at a very real level, subjects of the emperor, the truth was that there was one of greater importance than the Roman ruler. *Jesus* was the Messiah and the true "King of kings, and Lord of lords" (Rev 19:16). To put it another way, Jesus was the "Emperor of emperors." The one ruling in Rome was inferior, as was his kingdom, to the true monarch of the world.

So how was one to live as a subject of Rome while being a citizen of God's kingdom? Two ways. First, the Christians were to live as obedient and model citizens in their community. Whether they were formal citizens of the Roman Empire or not, the New Testament's authors exhorted the Christian community to be compliant members of the community. As such, they were to pay their taxes and honor their government leaders (Rom 13:6–7). They were to pray for their kings and those in authority over them (1 Tim 2:2) as they went about living quiet and peaceful lives (1 Thess 4:11; 1 Tim 2:2).

Second, the believers were to recognize there was a limit to their Roman loyalty. While it was appropriate to "give to Caesar what is Caesar's," it was also incumbent upon them to "give to God what is God's" (Mark 12:16). There were times in the first century, and ever since, when believers were confronted with the tension of the two competing kingdoms. In the growth of the early church, for example, authorities told Peter and John on multiple occasions, to remain silent in regard to their proclamation of Jesus (Acts 4:18; 5:28). In this regard, however, they would not concede to the earthly authorities and their loyalty to God came to the fore. When commanded to refrain from preaching the gospel, Peter and the apostles

---

7. Paul sometimes used his rights of citizenship (Acts 22:22–29; 25:10–11), and at other times voluntarily remained silent in regard to them (Acts 16:22–23, 37).

replied, "We must obey God rather than human beings!" (Acts 5:29). While they had obligations to the kingdom of Rome, they had a greater loyalty to the kingdom of God.

In a similar manner to the apostles, the believers in first-century Philippi felt the tension of living with a type of dual citizenship between the kingdoms of Rome and of God. The city of Philippi, commonly referred to as "little Rome," was a colonial outpost of Rome (Acts 16:12). In the city's history a Roman victory in battle resulted in many veteran soldiers retiring there.[8] The net result of this was that the city was established as a settlement which mirrored its larger capital. As a colony of Rome it was, no pun intended, a bit of Rome away from Rome. People dressed, ate, and acted as though they were present in Rome. As a colony, they were a visible outpost that epitomized what being Roman was like. It is against this cultural backdrop of citizenship that Paul wrote to the Philippians:

> Join together in following my example, brothers and sisters, and just as you have us as a model, keep your eyes on those who live as we do. For, as I have often told you before and now tell you again even with tears, many live as enemies of the cross of Christ. Their destiny is destruction, their god is their stomach, and their glory is in their shame. Their mind is set on earthly things. *But our citizenship is in heaven.* And we eagerly await a Savior from there, the Lord Jesus Christ. (Phil 3:17–21)

In this passage of Scripture Paul utilizes the term "citizenship" by moving it from a reference to Roman on to Christian identity. In these verses he gives both positive and negative ways of living in order to clarify and contrast the tension between earthly and heavenly citizenships. He urges his readers to follow his positive "example" (3:17) in contrast to the negative example of many who "live as enemies of the cross" (3:18). The phrase "their god is their stomach" (3:19) indicates that there were individuals who were living only for the here and now as seen in the temporary nature of their focus. Rather than focusing on things of lasting value these "enemies of the cross" are focused on the transitory and fleeting "earthly things" like their next meal. In contrast to this he exhorts believers to focus on the reality that their "citizenship is in heaven" (3:20).

The word translated "citizenship" carries with it the idea of one's membership in a "commonwealth" and "often denotes a colony of foreigners or

---

8. Fantin, *The Lord of the Entire World*, 146.

relocated veterans."⁹ Paul's use of this term almost certainly struck a chord with the many who connected it with Roman citizenship. Just as Philippi represented an extension of the commonwealth of Rome, so likewise the believers were to see themselves as a colonial outpost of God's coming kingdom. The idea could be translated, "Our home is in heaven, and on earth we are a colony of heavenly citizens."¹⁰

In Philippi not everybody was necessarily a citizen of Rome. Indeed, statistically even with the large Roman influence on the city the majority of the audience were likely not to be formal citizens of the Roman Empire. In spite of this, however, this passage firmly establishes, by way of the "citizenship" metaphor, that the believer in Christ has a formal connection with the kingdom of heaven. As such, the Philippians were to live as ambassadors of the kingdom of God while living as subjects of Rome. In a very real sense, the way Christians were to act, speak, and dress should have demonstrated to which kingdom they belonged. They were, in a sense, a little bit of heaven on earth.

WHAT CAN WE LEARN FROM THE METAPHOR OF CITIZENSHIP?

During the 1990s I had the great chance to live in the wonderful city of Chicago. During those years I fully embraced life as a Chicagoan. I ate deep-dish pizza, I supported the Cubs, and I even watched Michael Jordan play basketball in his prime. Though I am an Australian by birth, for a short season of my life I was a genuine Chicagoan. One year I made the long journey from Chicago back to Australia for the summer break. It was nice to return from the freezing shores of Lake Michigan to the warmer towns of my homeland. On one occasion while home in Australia I went for a country drive with my parents. We stopped at a small town for a break and then it was my turn to drive. I promptly jumped in the car and had driven about five hundred meters down the road when my father said, "You are going to drive on the correct side of the road, aren't you?" I then realized that I had, for about half a kilometer, been driving on the wrong side of the road. Fortunately it was rural Australia and there was no traffic. It became clear to me that living in America had changed me. While I was Australian, I had developed an impulse to move to the opposite side of the road.

9. BDAG, 845.
10. Ibid.

The Christian as Citizen

Feeling the tension between where we are from and where we are going is a very real dilemma for the Christian. Though I am a child of God and my citizenship and loyalty lie with the kingdom of heaven and its king Jesus, I still have natural impulses that pull me in the wrong direction. The Bible reveals that this inclination is the result of our fallen condition. Our natural disposition is not to serve God but to live in the way of this "world." When we are "born again," however, we receive new citizenship. There is a change of identity, a fresh start, and new loyalties generated. Paul summarizes this when he says:

> He has rescued us from the dominion of darkness and brought us into the kingdom of the Son he loves. (Col 1:15)

> Anyone who belongs to Christ has become a new person. The old life is gone; a new life has begun! (2 Cor 5:17, NLT)

When we give our lives to follow Christ, the Spirit of God grants us new birth. As a result we find that our values, desires, and allegiances change. We no longer live to serve our own pleasures; rather, we are now subservient to Christ and his kingdom. In light of this reality of our heavenly "citizenship," how then shall we live?

Recognize the Tension of Being a Dual Citizen

While we now serve Christ and his kingdom we live in the phase of history between the first and second comings of Christ. Jesus inaugurated his kingdom while upon earth and is truly the king of the world. Although he is rightfully the king, however, not everyone currently recognizes this sovereignty. In his generous grace God has allowed a time for people to turn from old ways and to submit to Jesus' kingship. In spite of this, however, people continue to rage against God and against his anointed servant Jesus. This rebellion will one day be quashed when Christ returns in victory to rule and reign over all of creation.

The tension for us, like those in the first century, is that we live in a world which refuses to bow its knee to Christ. Now, as then, people fail to submit to his rule, his voice, and his presence in their lives. The challenge for those of us in Christ, however, is that our natural disposition is also to reject God. Even though we are "in Christ," often in our lives we fail to live in light of the reality of God's kingdom. When we follow the sinful promptings of our heart we seek to live independently of God and fail to live in light of our citizenship.

When I was a child there used to be a saying that one could be "so *heavenly minded* that they are no *earthly* good." The idea was that a person could be so focused on "spiritual things" that they could neglect the reality of this world. Truth be told, however, our disposition actually reflects that we are usually "so *earthly minded* that we are no *heavenly* good." Our desires and our actions often reveal that our allegiance is not so much for Christ's kingdom as for the kingdom of this world. We live for the bigger house, the better holiday, the more comfortable retirement. We live as if our prime citizenship is the here and now.

In his book *Don't Waste Your Life*, John Piper describes how tragic it is when we live with an unhealthy preoccupation with the kingdom of this world. He writes:

> I will tell you what a tragedy is. I will show you how to waste your life. Consider a story from the February 1998 edition of *Reader's Digest*, which tells about a couple who "took early retirement from their jobs in the Northeast five years ago when he was 59 and she was 51. Now they live in Punta Gorda, Florida, where they cruise on their 30-foot trawler, play softball and collect shells."
>
> At first, when I read it I thought it might be a joke. A spoof on the American Dream. But it wasn't. Tragically, this was the dream: Come to the end of your life—your one-and-only precious, God-given life—and let the last great work of your life, before you give an account to your Creator, be this: playing softball and collecting shells.
>
> Picture them before Christ at the great day of judgment: "Look, Lord. See my shells." That is a tragedy. And people today are spending billions of dollars to persuade you to embrace that tragic dream. Over against that, I put my protest: Don't buy it. Don't waste your life.[11]

Far too often we chase after shells. We forget who we are, where we are going, and for whose glory we live. Our great pitfall is that we live for this day and this kingdom rather than for the kingdom that will not end.

As citizens of "Rome" it is easy to lose focus and think this is as good as it gets. We live, however, as dual citizens. While we do have a residence and domicile in this world, we are not of this world (John 17:16). When you're tempted to listen to the voice of Rome when it calls you to spend

---

11. Piper, *Don't Waste Your Life*, 45–46.

money on your own comforts remember your heavenly citizenship. When you're tempted by Rome to pursue sexual pleasure outside of God's will remember your heavenly citizenship. When you're tempted to speak falsely against a neighbor or to lie, remember your heavenly citizenship. There will be times when we fail and live according to the pattern of Rome rather than heaven. God, however, offers us his forgiveness as we struggle forward until the day when the one who began the good work in us will faithfully complete it.

The former African slave trader, John Newton, comprehended this truth. As he examined his life and reflected on his natural and his heavenly citizenship, he understood that while there was struggle God was still at work. When thinking about his past identity, as well as his future hope, he wrote:

> Though I am not what I ought to be, what I wish to be, and what I hope to be—yet I can truly say, I am not what I once was—a slave to sin and Satan! I can heartily join with the apostle and acknowledge, "By the grace of God—I am what I am!"[12]

As long as you live in this world you will face the tension of dual citizenship, but keep reminding yourself of who you are. You are a citizen of heaven.

Our Prime Allegiance Should Be Our Heavenly Citizenship

The metaphor of citizenship reminds us that while we have a tension of dual citizenship our *prime* allegiance must lie with the kingdom of God, that is the kingdom of "heaven." Now on a surface level this statement seems quite obvious. Almost all of us, who profess Christ, would make the claim that we are a heavenly people. In practice, however, our behavior doesn't always reflect this.

In the history of the church people have, at times, placed greater value on their national heritage and cultural identity than on their heavenly citizenship. While there is nothing inherently wrong in being proud of one's heritage or cultural background this should never be the defining mark of one's identity. I am not a Christian Australian. I am a Christian who happens to have been born in Australia. Now don't get me wrong, I love Australia. I'm fond of our land where our beaches are second to none. Meat

---

12. *John Newton as quoted by Winks, The Christian Pioneer, 84.*

pies, days at the cricket, barbeques in the summer, and camping in the bush are alright with me. Australia, in my opinion, is still the best place in the world to live. However, at the end of the day, this is not ultimately or even primarily my homeland. Like Abraham and the saints of old, I'm living and longing for "a better country—a heavenly one" (Heb 11:16).

Patriotism has its place in culture and we should certainly not despise our backgrounds, but nor should we make too much of them. Unfortunately, in my experience I have seen too many Christians at sporting events enthusiastically singing with hands on their heart and tears in their eyes as the national anthem plays, only to see the same Christians barely awake, singing with very little emotion about the living God on a Sunday morning at church. I know many Christians who love to talk about the political landscape of their country with deep passion and conviction, yet that same passion is almost absent when talking about the Scriptures or what God is doing in their lives. Now while it is good and appropriate for us to be committed members of our society, we must always keep in perspective the bigger picture as to our allegiance. Our prime allegiance is our *heavenly citizenship*, not the geographical country we are temporarily residing in.

In the early church the issue of a citizenship in heaven was something they needed to be reminded of. In several of the letters of the New Testament, the authors addressed issues of division surrounding the role of cultural heritage. In Acts 15, for example, questions arose from the Jewish leadership as to whether Gentiles must conform to Jewish behavior in order to be fully embraced as God's people. There were obviously people who believed Gentiles needed extra grace to become part of God's people. On the other hand, some Gentiles who originally were not part of God's people and were "grafted in" seemed to have made the mistake of downplaying the significance of God's people Israel (cf. Rom 9:17–24).

The Jew/Gentile tension in the early church was significant. Rather than downplaying these cultural backgrounds, Paul, who was both Jewish and an apostle to the Gentiles, called the groups to recognize that they were part of "one new humanity" (Eph 2:15). I honestly don't think Paul was interested in people identifying themselves as Jewish, Roman, or Greek believers. They were "children of God" and members of one family. To those of Gentile background he reminded them that they were now "no longer foreigners and strangers, but *fellow citizens* with God's people and also members of his household" (Eph 2:19). Paul reveals that this new citizenship was a mystery. He explains:

> This mystery is that through the gospel the Gentiles are heirs together with Israel, members together of one body, and sharers together in the promise in Christ Jesus. (Eph 3:6)

This may be shocking to you, but God doesn't view you as an American Christian, or as a Jewish Christian, a Chinese or a British Christian. He views you as a citizen of his kingdom. Rather than finding identity in our cultural heritage, which will soon be forgotten, the Scriptures calls us to regard and celebrate our *prime* allegiance to the kingdom that will never pass away.

If anyone could identify his ethic citizenship and national identity it would have been Paul.[13] He was "circumcised on the eighth day, of the people of Israel, of the tribe of Benjamin, a Hebrew of Hebrews" (Phil 3:5). Yet nowhere do we find Paul describing himself as a "Jewish Christian," a "Tarsian Christian," or even a "Roman Christian." Paul was not primarily committed to the fading cultural markers of earthly citizenship. Rather, he wanted to "know Christ" (Phil 3:10) and find his boast in him. That meant living with an awareness that his loyalty lay with his heavenly citizenship. We would do well to learn from Paul's example as we prioritize Christ's kingdom rather than the cultural one we happen to be living in.

Our Collective Citizenship Should Point to the Kingdom of God

One of the things that I love to do is travel. Over the years I have had the opportunity to travel to over forty countries. The thing I love about travel, apart from the diversity of food, is meeting other members of God's family throughout. Over the years I've sung, prayed, listened, learned, cried, and laughed with believers in places like Nepal, Ecuador, India, England, Argentina, and the Solomon Islands. From mud-hut churches to gatherings in thousand-year-old cathedrals, from meeting with a small group of Maori believers in the far north of New Zealand to a large group gathering in Texas—all over the world I've discovered a special unity exists when God's people come together around the person of the Lord Jesus Christ. While there are some terrific international clubs and organizations out there, there is nothing that comes close to the marvel of seeing the diverse body of Christ in the Christian church.

---

13. The only time Paul appealed to his Roman citizenship was when facing an illegal trial (Acts 22:25). Even in this context of trials, however, he didn't always make his citizenship known (cf. Acts 16:22–23, 37).

There is great power when the church exemplifies its God-ordained function. When God's people, as diverse as they are, come together in unity it is quite astonishing to an outside world. Paul knew and understood this and that is why the "citizenship" metaphor is so apt. Just as Philippi had an obvious connection to Rome, as seen through the city's food, culture, and practice, so the Christian community should provide an equally obvious connection to the heavenly community to which it belongs. When the Christian church functions as it should, people should get a taste of what God's kingdom is really like. While the church is not perfect, it is a preview of coming attractions. It is an earthly snapshot of a heavenly reality.

Now we all recognize that the church is made up of imperfect people. Someone has said, "If you find the perfect church, don't join it! The moment you do, it will be ruined." We all know the church has failed in many realms. Unfortunately the history of the church is littered with abominable abuses of power and sinful behavior that have damaged many. Time and again we read of people injured, abused, and damaged by wicked people who have identified themselves as Christ followers. Not to minimize the pain of those hurt by the church, but a look at the church also reveals that millions of lives have been healed, restored, and embraced when authentic believers seeking to live for Christ have sought to obey his call. When the church has loved, served, aided, and embraced the downtrodden it has preached loudly the love of God and the lordship of Christ.

The question for you and me is that as people look at our churches, would they say we have been a voice of hope, and light, and life? Would our behavior both at an individual level and our corporate Christian gatherings reveal that we are different types of citizens? Would they look at us and make the connection that we belong to another place, another kingdom, a heavenly kingdom?

Heavenly citizenship should motivate us to live in a way worthy of the gospel. Jesus told his disciples to "let your light shine before others, that they may *see* your good deeds and glorify your Father in heaven" (Matt 5:16). In a similar manner Paul exhorted the Philippians to "do everything without grumbling or arguing" so that they would "become blameless and pure, children of God without fault in a warped and crooked generation" (Phil 2:14–15). The result would be that the church would shine "like stars in the sky" (Phil 2:16). When the church lives up to its heavenly mandate, the gospel is loudly proclaimed.

CHRISTIAN CITIZENS

The citizenship metaphor reminds us of our core identity. As we have observed, we are all born as citizens of Rome. That is, before Christ, our identity is squarely connected to the world. When we trust in Christ, however, we are granted a new citizenship, a heavenly one. The net result of our new citizenship is that we now live, act, and speak as "ambassadors of Christ" (2 Cor 5:20). Though we experience a type of dual citizenship now, the day will come when we will join with all of God's people who have lived through the ages in the kingdom that will know no end. With eager hearts we look forward to that day because, as Augustine puts it, "Incomparably more glorious than Rome, is that heavenly city in which for victory you have truth; for dignity, holiness; for peace, felicity; for life, eternity."[14]

---

14. Augustine, *City of God*, 2:29 (McCracken, trans.).

REFLECTIONS

1. What stands out to you about the Christian being likened to a *citizen*? What in this image is either new to you, or a helpful reminder?
2. What are some of the character traits that should reflect someone who is a citizen of heaven?
3. How should the reality of the coming kingdom of God impact your daily decisions such as relationships, finances, career, etc.?
4. What do you find most challenging in living as a dual citizen of God's kingdom and the kingdom of this world?

PRAYER

> Wonderful King,
>
> We come to you as citizens of your kingdom with gratefulness and humility. You are a kind and benevolent king. Thank you for calling us to be your subjects. We willingly and joyfully delight in your lordship, and ask that you would empower us to live in such a way that we reflect the glory of your coming kingdom. Forgive us for too tightly aligning ourselves with the kingdom of this world. Transform our hearts and lift our eyes so that we would live today in light of what will be. We look forward earnestly to the day when your kingdom will come and your will shall be done on earth as it is in heaven. Until that time help us to be good and godly citizens, for King Jesus' sake.
>
> Amen.

4

The Christian as Combatant

> "Fight the good fight of faith."
> —1 TIMOTHY 6:12

LOVE HIM OR HATE him "Iron" Mike Tyson will go down in boxing folklore as one of the all-time greats. A junior Olympic gold medalist, Tyson became the youngest heavyweight champion in the history of boxing at the age of just twenty. In his prime Iron Mike struck fear into the heart of even the most valiant of competitors. He would enter the ring with minimal fanfare, but his menacing stares along with the occasional growl made it obvious he was not there for a church picnic. Not a big man, by heavyweight standards, what Tyson lacked in size he made up for with his aggression. Indeed, Iron Mike's hostility is what has made him infamous when, during one title fight, he failed to curb his passion and overstepped the rules by biting off part of the ear of an opponent. Iron Mike: a mean hombre, a tough combatant, a fearless fighter, and a renowned boxer.

The sport of boxing is nothing new. From the dawn of time there have always been grown men, like Mike Tyson, who have expended energy trying to knock the other down. In 648 BC, for example, the sport of *Pankration*, a mixture of boxing and wrestling, was introduced to the Olympic Games. In this ancient type of martial art the competitors would grapple each other using shoulder locks, arm bars, and choking techniques with the goal of causing the opponent to pass out or submit. Although there were loose rules, such as no biting, the men were free to use whatever technique they saw fit to defeat their rival. Men displayed their physical prowess as well as their mental acumen as they sought to outmuscle and outwit their opponent, often in front of large crowds. Not every contest, however, was waged in the Olympic ring. Speaking of unsanctioned brawls among those of ill repute Philo records:

> For what the athletes do in the arena while sober, in the daylight, with the eyes of all Greece upon then, in the hope of victory and the crown and in the exercise of their skill, are debased by the revelers who ply their activities in convivial gatherings by night and in darkness, drink-besotted, ignorant and skillful only for mischief to inflict dishonour, insult and grievous outrage on the objects of their assault. And if no one plays the umpire and comes forward to intervene and separate them they carry on the bout with increased license to the finish, ready both to kill and be killed.[1]

In the ancient world people fought one another. Sometimes this took place in the arena, and at other times on the street. Physical combat, however, was not just an ancient world activity, but can also be found in our own modern context. Though *Pankration* has not been embraced in the modern Olympic Games, boxing and mixed martial arts continue to be widely practiced as competitive sports and are watched by millions. In the "octagon" of the Ultimate Fighting Championship (UFC), for example, athletes wrestle, punch, throw, choke, and kick in a manner reminiscent of the ancient Greek *Pankration*. This relatively gruesome sport is watched in over 150 countries and is a multimillion-dollar industry. The massive interest in UFC, alongside boxing and professional wrestling, demonstrates clearly that people are still attracted to combative physical sport. Indeed, it is this desire for physical combat that is the thematic base of the cult classic film *The Fight Club* starring Brad Pitt.

Now I recognize that boxing may not be a sport you have an affinity with. The idea of two mature adults strapping on gloves and slugging it out may actually be repulsive to you, but it is this combative image of struggle, fighting, and battle that the New Testament, on more than one occasion, uses to describe aspects of the Christian life. Now the fact that the New Testament uses language of struggle and fight might give you the wrong impression. Let me first clarify what the New Testament does *not* say. Nowhere in the New Testament is the physical harm of others condoned.

1. Philo, *Contemplative Life*, 42–43 (Colson, trans.).

Indeed, Jesus said, "If anyone slaps you on the right cheek, turn to them the other cheek also" (Matt 5:39) and "all who draw the sword will die by the sword" (Matt 26:52). Physically pounding someone into submission, or worse, is not on Jesus' discipleship agenda. So why do the New Testament authors provide combative images of their day to describe the Christian life? As we will see, the writers of the New Testament will show us how the *discipline* that forms the basis of *Pankration* and ancient boxing is a character trait that the followers of Jesus would do well to imitate to be skilled combatants in the spiritual life.

THE CHRISTIAN AS A DISCIPLINED COMBATANT

Discipline is just plain hard work. It is, however, almost always the companion of those who would succeed in a particular area of life. People do not simply roll out of bed and become concert pianists. First, they spend hours learning to sight-read music and practice pieces, and practicing their "scales." People do not run marathons without first having prepared months in advance through a disciplined regime of shorter runs as they build up to the forty-two kilometer test of endurance. People do not master a language by simply attending a one-day seminar; rather, they do it through memorizing paradigms, engaging in conversation, and forcing themselves to speak in the language. Most skills in life require attention, practice, and discipline.

What is true in other areas of life is also true of the Christian life. Growth in the Christian life does not just happen automatically; it requires a large dose of self-control and spiritual regulation. To grow spiritually, like growing physically, requires a good consistent diet along with healthy exercise. A child that has a poor diet and isn't physically active will likely be stunted in growth and face problems as an adult. In a similar manner, the Christian who doesn't nourish themselves through a disciplined lifestyle of feeding on God's word and actively using their spiritual gifts to bless the body of Christ will likely not mature into an effective disciple of Jesus. In the early church this seems have been a problem. We read:

> I gave you milk, not solid food, for you were not yet ready for it. Indeed, you are still not ready. (1 Cor 3:2)

Knowing Who You Are

> In fact, though by this time you ought to be teachers, you need someone to teach you the elementary truths of God's word all over again. You need milk, not solid food! (Heb 5:12)

Rather than maturing in Christ, it appears that many within the early community of believers resembled spiritual infants.

The antidote to spiritual immaturity is the intentional and disciplined life. The one who would grow needs discipline. This idea is expressed by the author of Hebrews, who exhorted his readers to "watch your *life* and *doctrine* closely. Persevere in them, because if you do, you will save both yourself and your hearers" (Heb 13:2).

In this verse the author is reminding his audience, and by extension us, of two things that are required for growth in Christ. First, we need to pay attention to our "life," that is our behavior, the way we think, act, and speak. Second, we need to pay attention to our "doctrine," that is, what we believe about God, our world, and ourselves. In essence, we need a measured, regulated, self-controlled approach to our spiritual life. What we need is spiritual *discipline*. So what does that look like? To illustrate what it's like Paul writes that we ought to be disciplined like a runner and a boxer. In 1 Cor 9:24–27 we read:

> Do you not know that in a race all the runners run, but only one gets the prize? Run in such a way as to get the prize. Everyone who competes in the games goes into strict training. They do it to get a crown that will not last, but we do it to get a crown that will last forever. Therefore I do not run like someone running aimlessly; I do not fight like a boxer beating the air. No, I strike a blow to my body and make it my slave so that after I have preached to others, I myself will not be disqualified for the prize.

The cultural background of Paul's use of the athletic and boxing metaphors in 1 Corinthians 9 undoubtedly lies in the Greek Isthmian games that were held not many miles from Corinth. The Isthmian games were a large sporting spectacle held every two years. It was second in size only to the Olympics and included a variety of events such as wrestling, javelin throwing, foot races, and boxing. The Greeks loved their sports and athletes were held in high esteem in the community. While the Jews were not a sport-loving people, the Apostle Paul nevertheless capitalized on the popular sporting images of the Isthmian games when he wrote these words to encourage the Christians to think about their own spiritual life.

A Disciplined Focus

Paul observes that an athlete trains with the goal of competing to "get the prize" (9:24). In this metaphor he pictures a runner who has a clear purpose as to his pursuit. He runs, not for the sake of leisure, but with the goal of attaining his desired outcome, namely, victory. Athletes in the Isthmian games knew what their tasks were. If one were competing in a foot race, it was to cross the line first. If one were throwing, it was to launch the javelin the furthest. If one were boxing or wrestling, it was to bring the opponent into submission. The goal was to "get the prize" (9:24).

The "prize" (9:24) in the Corinthian context was a "perishable wreath" (9:25). The winning athlete would be awarded a headpiece that was made of parsley or celery or pine. Not really our idea of a great trophy to put on the mantelpiece, but something in the ancient world that represented hard work and reward. The reward, however, was not simply about the "perishable wreath," it was the resultant glory that would accompany the victory. The Greek philosopher and historian Dio Chrysostom, having witnessed such victory ceremonies, wrote:

> The noble man holds his hardships to be his greatest antagonists, and with them he is ever wont to battle day and night, not to win a sprig of parsley as so many goats might do, nor for a bit of wild olive, or of pine, but to win happiness and virtue throughout all the days of his life.[2]

To win the prize meant to win fame and fortune. Paul's point is that the disciplined athlete needs to be focused on the end goal. The runner needs to focus on the finish line and the boxer on finishing his opponent.

Having exhorted the Christian to be like a runner or boxer who competes with an eye on the "prize," Paul next explains how Christians are *unlike* the ancient athletes. While we are to compete and be disciplined like the ancient runner and boxer, our "prize" is not simply a temporal reward that perishes and withers away, but ours is long lasting. An athlete competes "to get a crown that will not last . . . we do it to get a crown that lasts for ever" (9:25). Gordon Fee explains:

> The runner, of course, had no thought for the composition of the "crown." As with modern athletes, victory meant fame, prestige, and sometimes fortune. The "crown" was the symbol of victory; if

---

2. *Discourses*, 8.15 (Cohoon, trans.).

it faded, the fame that followed was often more enduring. But even that means nothing in light of the believer's crown.[3]

In the history of boxing there have been many famous champions, but perhaps none has been more so than the colorful and controversial Muhammad Ali. Muhammad Ali was once a household name, a great competitor and champion over many years. Once. Sadly the former champion now cuts a lonely figure as he lives with Parkinson's disease. Were you to ask the average twenty-year-old about Muhammad Ali, or any of the other great champions like Rocky Marciano, George Forman, or Sugar Ray Leonard, you would probably just get a blank stare. They would most likely respond with, "who?" That is the nature of sport and fame. The crown of the modern day athlete, along with their accompanying fame and fortune, is quickly forgotten as new athletes rise up to take the places of previous ones.

The nature of an athlete's prize is fleeting, but not so for the prize attained by the servant of God. The Scriptures consistently talk about the longevity of the righteous' reward. For example:

> Those who are wise will shine like the brightness of the heavens, and those who lead many to righteousness, like the stars *for ever and ever.* (Dan 12:3)

> The world and its desires pass away, but whoever does the will of God *lives forever.* (1 John 2:17)

Unlike the ephemeral "crown" presented by a civic dignitary, the servant of God lives to please God and receive the "crown" that doesn't fade. As the Scriptures reminds us:

> Now there is in store for me the *crown of righteousness*, which the Lord, the righteous Judge, will award to me on that day—and not only to me, but also to all who have longed for his appearing. (2 Tim 4:8)

> Blessed is the one who perseveres under trial because, having stood the test, that person will receive the *crown of life* that the Lord has promised to those who love him. (Jam 1:12)

> And when the Chief Shepherd appears, you will receive the *crown of glory* that will never fade away. (1 Pet 5:4)

---

3. Fee, *Corinthians*, 437.

The Christian as Combatant

The boxer at the Isthmian games had focus. Likewise we are to imitate such focus-driven discipline in our lives as we live for the unfading "prize."

A Disciplined Preparation

Paul also reveals that, like a boxer, Christians are to be disciplined in their preparation. He writes, "Everyone who competes in the games goes into *strict training*" (1 Cor 9:25). In the ancient world, as with ours, there was a "no pain, no gain" mentality. Just as a modern-day boxer endlessly jumps rope, runs miles on the street, and punches bags until his arms feel like jelly, so the ancient boxer also needed long and sustained preparation for the games. Paul states that "everyone" who competes goes into strict training. To make it to the Olympic or Isthmian games was not something one just signed up for. Boxers would adopt strict diets to maximize their strength. They would live disciplined lives in regard to what they would eat, or not eat.[4] No junk food, no excesses of wines, and no sweets for these warriors. To be at their peak they would be disciplined in their selection of food. They would also, in preparation for the games, be disciplined in how they approached their sexual appetites.[5] The athlete would seek to remove any and all distractions in order to train well and, upon the beginning of the games, they would swear allegiance to Zeus by publicly declaring the fact that they had trained for ten months prior to the games.[6]

The training of the boxer was not always pleasant. Seneca, the Roman philosopher and statesman, explains this when he uses a boxer's training to inspire a friend to live a virtuous life. He writes:

> What blows do athletes receive on their faces and all over their bodies! Nevertheless, through their desire for fame they endure torture, and they undergo these things not only because they are fighting but in order to be able to fight. *Their very training means torture.* So let us also win the way to victory in all our struggles, for the reward is not a garland or a palm or a trumpeter who calls for silence at the proclamation of our names, but rather virtue, steadfastness of soul, and a peace that is won for all time.[7]

---

4. See, for example, Epictetus, *Discourses*, 3.10.10.

5. There are examples of people refraining from sex so they could focus on their Olympic ambition. See Plato, *Laws*, 840a.

6. Pausanias, *Description of Greece*, 9.24.9

7. Seneca, *Moral Epistles*, 78.16 (Gummer, trans.).

In a similar description the rhetorician Lucian wrote of the pain involved for those wanting to use the boxing arena as a platform to fame and fortune. Addressing a friend about why the "prize" of a wreath made of celery or parsley was worthwhile to the contestant he explained:

> My dear fellow, it is not the bare gifts that we have in view! These are merely tokens of the victory and marks to identify the winners. But the reputation that goes with them is worth everything to the victors, and to attain it, even to be kicked is nothing to men who seek to capture fame through hardships. *Without hardships it cannot be acquired*; the man who covets it must put up with many unpleasantnesses in the beginning before at last he can expect the profitable and delightful outcome of his exertions.[8]

For the boxer to be competitive, to be fit for the fight, to win the prize and defeat his opponent required not just aspirations, but physically demanding work. Discipline involved "hardships" that were unpleasant. The training was treacherous, but it put the boxer in good stead when the real fight was on.

For Paul, the boxer's discipline is really the key to the whole metaphor. For the Christian to mature in Christ means exercising discipline. To grow in godliness means saying "yes" to some things, but having the restraint to say "no" at other times. One does not roll out of bed one morning and suddenly attain godliness. The Christian life, like a boxer's, is about doing the little things regularly and well. It is about being disciplined enough to train oneself. The Scriptures remind us,

> *Train yourself* to be godly. For physical training is of some value, but godliness has value for all things, holding promise for both the present life and the life to come. (1 Tim 4:7b–8)

> Solid food is for the mature, who by constant use have *trained themselves* to distinguish good from evil. (Heb 5:14)

> No discipline seems pleasant at the time, but painful. Later on, however, it produces a harvest of righteousness and peace for those who have been *trained* by it. (Heb 12:11)

Paul's key theme in using the boxing metaphor is to remind us of the importance of keeping our focus on our eternal goal and disciplining ourselves to remain focused on this promised prize. But in the midst of this

---

8. Lucian, *Anacharchis*, 10 (Harmon, trans.).

positive use of the boxing metaphor, Paul offers also a sober warning to us, again by way of the boxer.

The Danger of Ill Discipline

Iron Mike Tyson's first defeat as a boxer came as a complete surprise. Having risen to the top of the boxing world, Tyson held the WBC, WBA, and IBF titles as he entered into the ring to face the relatively unknown James "Buster" Douglas in 1990. Douglas had a fairly checkered record in the ring having been knocked out several times in his lead up to the Tyson fight. Many believed that the Tyson vs. Douglas showdown was simply a warm-up fight to prepare Iron Mike for the real battle against Evander Holyfield. No one, however, communicated this to Buster Douglas, and subsequently the 42–1 underdog came out and floored Tyson, much to the amazement of the world.

While James "Buster" Douglas was billed as something of a "Rocky" type figure—the poor battler who overcomes all odds to win—the reality was that the fight said more about Mike Tyson's *lack* of preparation than Douglas's supremacy as a boxer. Douglas went on to lose his first defense and never regained the title. As far as technique, power, and ability go, Douglas was not half the fighter that Tyson was. This, however, is the tragedy of the story. Tyson, though a phenomenal athlete, a powerful puncher, and a world-class tactician, dropped his guard and failed to accomplish his goal. He underestimated his opponent, was *ill disciplined*, and subsequently lost his way. In the aftermath of Tyson's fight his life further unraveled and by the end of the following year he would find himself in prison on rape charges. Though he would later be released and go on to again find boxing fame, Iron Mike's story is one filled with pain and loss.

Ill discipline is something that no successful boxer can afford to have. To drop one's guard, to pack on too much weight, or to refrain from studying an opponent's tactics, will result in a professional boxer being defeated. In a similar manner, the Christian who neglects their spiritual life through ill discipline, often shown in apathy toward the Scriptures, prayer, and fellowship with God's people, will not only fail to mature, but often will fall back into spiritual despair. It is this spiritual despair that the Apostle Paul wants to avoid, and wants to save us from when he writes;

> I do not fight like a boxer beating the air. I strike a blow to my
> body and make it my slave so that after I have preached to others,
> I myself will not be disqualified for the prize. (1 Cor 9:26b–27)

The idea of a "boxer beating the air" points to the futility of what we now call "shadow boxing." Philo of Alexandria, writing in the first century, likens his philosophical opponents to shadow boxers when he writes, "they are boxers who win admiration in a mock encounter among themselves and are thought very little of when they engage in a match."[9] While it might look impressive to have fast moving feet, swift hands, and good technique, at the end of the day punching air is quite an easy feat. Indeed, even children can shadow box effectively! A boxer "beating the air" is not going to accomplish much.

Suppose a professional boxer entered into the ring and at the sound of the bell remained in his corner and just started wildly swinging his arms in the air while his opponent stood in the center of the ring waiting for him to come forward. It would be foolish for the fighter to expend unnecessary energy without actually landing any blows on his rival. He might look impressive and stylish, but if he doesn't engage in the fight his effort will be in vain. Paul does not want himself, or the reader, to be like one of these shadow boxers. He does not want himself or the believing community to be ill disciplined and lacking focus. In contrast, boxing to win the prize means keeping focused on the task at hand.

So how does Paul execute his goal and avoid aimlessly boxing? He tells us in verse 27. He does it through *discipline*. Continuing his boxing metaphor he says, "I strike a blow to my body." The word "blow" literally means "to blacken the eye, give a black eye, strike in the face."[10] Paul wants to deal a powerful blow to his rival, but interestingly the opponent in this context is not an outsider, not a fellow minister, or even a member of the congregation; rather, he wants to strike himself. Now what Paul is *not* implying is some form of ancient asceticism where one flagellates oneself. Rather, he is using the metaphor to say that he willingly submits himself to hardship and even difficulty in ministry because of his strong desire to win "the prize."

Paul exercised disciplined restraint in the way that he lived. A practical example of this can be observed in the way he viewed being remunerated for his service. In 1 Cor 9:12 Paul explains that even though he had rights to receive support, to prove his motivation for ministry he was content to

---

9. Philo, *The Worse Attacks Are Better*, 45 (Colson and Whitaker, trans.).
10. BDAG, 1043.

go without. We read, "If others have this right of [financial] support from you, shouldn't we have it all the more? *But we did not use this right.* On the contrary, we put up with anything rather than hinder the gospel of Christ."

As an apostle and vocational minister of God's word Paul had every right to ask for financial payment for his ministry. Even though he was free to earn a living from the gospel, however, he chose to work with his hands because he wanted to honor God and live for the prize. It was no doubt hard for Paul to make tents by day and preach by night. He would have been well within his rights as an apostle to verbally chastise the Corinthians and even demand financial support, yet he *intentionally* chose to endure such spiritual blows because he wanted to remain focused on preaching the gospel. In enduring hardship Paul was not seeking the accolades of his fellowman; rather, he showed personal restraint in order to please God.

A final motivating factor in Paul's metaphor of the boxer is the possibility of disqualification. Paul didn't want to be prohibited from winning the prize on the basis of spiritual failure. For Paul the possibility of moral and spiritual failure was always a reality. For Paul, and all of us, sin is an ever-present threat to our spiritual growth. Just as a boxer was obligated to live within the constraints of the boxing code, so the Christian must seek to carefully follow the law of Christ in personal holiness. Now some have pressed this issue too far and found themselves distracted by issues over whether Paul is advocating the idea of disqualification to include "losing one's salvation" but this is to miss the point. Paul is not using disqualification in the context of whether or not one gets into heaven as much as he is using his metaphor to give a strong pastoral exhortation to obey.[11] We should feel tension over Paul's exhortation. If the great apostle was concerned about failure in his spiritual life so should we be.

Paul was concerned about the consequences of ill discipline. He loved the Corinthians too much to let them slide into spiritual apathy so he exhorted them strongly. On the negative, he warned them of spiritual disqualification. On the positive, he gave the antidote to failure: namely, developing a spiritually disciplined lifestyle.

WHAT CAN WE LEARN FROM THE BOXER?

Boxing in the ancient world was a commonly practiced sport found most typically in the Olympic and Isthmian games. Though the New Testament

---

11. For further reflections on this see, David Garland, *1 Corinthians*, 444–45.

does not condone this sport *per se*, it does use the metaphor of the boxer to help us think about our Christian identity. In particular, there are three lessons that the boxer can teach us.

1. Know What You Are Fighting For

First, as a follower of Jesus I need to know what I am fighting for. Just as the boxer fought to win a prize, both the perishable crown and the accompanying fame and fortune, so then as a Christian I am to look to win the prize that God has called me to. God has not called me to live for myself, but to live for his pleasure and purpose. The result of following God is the reward of knowing him and facing the joyous prospect of living with him forever. Unlike the boxer the Christian hope does not fade. As believers we need to consistently remind ourselves of this reward which won't perish. The New Testament regularly points us to this. Consider the following exhortations.

> Do not store up for yourselves treasures on earth, where moths and vermin destroy, and where thieves break in and steal. But *store up for yourselves treasures in heaven*, where moths and vermin do not destroy, and where thieves do not break in and steal. (Matt 6:19–20)

> Since, then, you have been raised with Christ, *set your hearts on things above*, where Christ is, seated at the right hand of God. *Set your minds on things above*, not on earthly things. (Col 3:1–2)

The world we live in tempts us to focus on the temporal rewards of the here and now. The media tells us happiness is found in a bigger home, a faster car, a nicer body, and a prosperous retirement fund. We pursue these things as if they were the "prize." When we do this, however, our attention moves off the real purposes of our existence. You and I have been created for God's delight and when we find our focus on joyfully pursuing him and his will we find that the real prize is knowing him. It is this singularity of mind that Paul had when he wrote:

> I press on to take hold of that for which Christ Jesus took hold of me. Brothers and sisters, I do not consider myself yet to have taken hold of it. But one thing I do: Forgetting what is behind and straining toward what is ahead, *I press on toward the goal to win the prize* for which God has called me heavenward in Christ Jesus. (Phil 3:12–13)

The Christian as Combatant

The boxer is calling us to know our goal. The boxer reminds us to know what it is we are fighting for.

2. Be Disciplined in Your Preparation for the Fight

Second, just as a boxer needs a disciplined diet, tactical plan, and physical fitness, so also the Christian needs to incorporate elements of spiritual discipline into their lifestyle if they are to mature in Christ. Just as the boxer needs to train himself to fight, so we also need to train ourselves in godliness. Paul relinquished many of his God-given rights as an apostle in order to be most effective. Paul restrained his behavior because he wanted to be useful in the service of God. He understood that disciplined spiritual training, through hard work, pays dividends. Elsewhere we read:

> For physical training is of some value, but godliness has value for all things, holding promise for both the present life and the life to come. (1 Tim 4:7b–8)

> No discipline seems pleasant at the time, but painful. Later on, however, it produces a harvest of righteousness and peace for those who have been trained by it. (Heb 12:11)

Spiritual maturity is not a one-off event; rather, Christian growth is an ongoing process that involves engaging with God regularly through reading and reflecting on the Scriptures, listening to God speak, speaking with him in prayer, and interacting with God's people. These all require time and effort. Many of these habits are unnatural to us yet they are critical if we are to grow into the people that God wants us to be. Just as I need to provide my children a well balanced diet of food if they are to physically flourish, so we need to nourish our souls through regular spiritual practices if we are to be well-rounded children of God.

3. Recognize the Possibility of Spiritual Failure

Third, like a boxer who can be disqualified, it is just not enough to know about the fight, we must also compete within the guidelines. Failure to understand the guidelines of the fight can equate to an inadequate preparation. This can result in our failure.

Toward the end of Paul's life many with whom he had served abandoned the fight through ill discipline. Demas, for example, "because he loved this world" deserted Paul and lost sight of the prize (2 Tim 4:10). Not wanting his young protégé Timothy to meet the same end, Paul charged his associate,

> Timothy, my son, I am giving you this command in keeping with the prophecies once made about you, so that by recalling them you may *fight the battle well*. (1 Tim 1:18)

> *Fight the good fight* of the faith. Take hold of the eternal life to which you were called when you made your good confession in the presence of many witnesses. (1 Tim. 6:12)

Just as a boxer can grow lazy, slow, and rest on their previous victories, we also as Christians can make the mistake of resting on our laurels and subsequently let down our guard. With an enemy that is always ready to devour us (1 Pet 5:8) we must remain diligent in our fight lest we lose sight of the prize. There will be times when we get knocked down. In fact, you may be reading this and feel that you have been disqualified because of a lack of discipline. While sin may continue to rain blows upon us, however, the good news of the gospel is that in Christ we have forgiveness. If we come in repentance and faith to the cross, our Master offers forgiveness and helps us back on our feet with the invitation to keep fighting.

May we learn from the boxer a discipline that enables us to fight in such a way as not to be disqualified, but in a way that we can win the crown and finish our days like Paul, who could say, "*I have fought the good fight*, I have finished the race, I have kept the faith" (2 Tim. 4:7).

The Christian as Combatant

REFLECTIONS

1. The ancient boxer fought so as to win a "prize." What would you describe as the "prize" for which Christians are to fight?
2. The boxer's life was one filled with discipline. What are some of the different aspects of Christian discipline?
3. What areas of Christian discipline do you find hardest? What are some small but practical ways you can develop discipline in these areas?
4. Spiritual defeat can be a common occurrence in the Christian experience. What roles do grace and forgiveness play in the life of the Christian?

PRAYER

> Gracious Master,
> We come to you not on the basis of our own strength or goodness, but we confidently stand before you because of the perfect work of your beloved Son the Lord Jesus Christ. As born-again children strengthen us, through your Holy Spirit, to move from spiritual infancy to maturity in Christ. Help us to keep our focus upon his renown as we live disciplined and restrained lives that fulfill your desires for this world. Forgive us for our ill discipline and restore us that we might live to honor your name. When discouraged, pick us up. When defeated, restore our spirit. When victorious, keep us humble. We pray this for the honor of the one who defeated sin and death, and lives and reigns in victory with you, and the Holy Spirit, one God, blessed forever.
> Amen.

5

The Christian as Farmer

"Remember this: Whoever sows sparingly will also reap sparingly, and whoever sows generously will also reap generously."

—2 CORINTHIANS 9:6

"Let us not become weary in doing good, for at the proper time we will reap a harvest if we do not give up."

—GALATIANS 6:9

IN JUNE 2013 THE British Nutrition Foundation surveyed 27,500 children on the origin of various foods. The results revealed that one child in ten thought that tomatoes grow underground, one child in five that fish fingers were made of chicken, and a staggering one in three believed cheese came from plants.[1] Clearly most children aren't aware of where their evening meals come from. Many children, it seems, assume food originates from the supermarket. The children, however, are not alone in their ignorance. With the development of large supermarkets, online shopping, and home-delivery services many adults are equally in the dark as to how and where their food is produced.

The ignorance common today as to the sourcing of food was certainly not a problem in the ancient world. In biblical times almost everybody

---

1. http://www.nutrition.org.uk/nutritioninthenews/pressreleases/healthyeatingweek

knew something about the land. People understood that if it didn't rain there would be no harvest. Most had a basic comprehension of grain, fruit, livestock, and soil. Indeed, whereas farming and general agriculture are known only by a segment of the population nowadays, up to 90 percent of the Roman Empire's workers were engaged in some type of farming or herding during New Testament times.[2]

Given the New Testament world's highly agricultural backdrop it should not surprise us to see a wide variety of farming metaphors being used in the writings of Scripture. Jesus, for example, speaks about landowners, sowing seed, using plows, tending vineyards, yoking animals, and threshing grain. Indeed most of Jesus' teachings in his parables assume a general awareness of the farming way of life. It is perhaps because of our lack of knowledge about the agrarian practices of the ancient world that we miss many important insights into the life portrayed in the farming metaphors. With this in mind, it would be useful to explore some agricultural metaphors and see what we learn from the life and work of the ancient farmer and how that relates to our Christian self-understanding.

THE FARMER SOWS IN THE HOPE OF REAPING

When I was midway through my high school years I was relatively unsure as to which career path I was going to take. I entertained several ideas: radio announcer, pilot, perhaps a customs officer. As I was contemplating these professions a new career suddenly entered my mind. After church one Sunday my parents dropped by a bakery to pick up something for lunch when the smell of warm, freshly baked bread awoke my senses and almost as if hypnotized I decided I should be a baker! I could, I reasoned to myself, make sausage rolls, meat pies, and crusty sourdough bread for soup for the rest of my days. As I chatted with an older friend about pursuing this career, however, I was highly disappointed to discover becoming a baker required very early morning starts, something I felt incapable of doing. Subsequently I scratched baker off my career options.

The process of making bread is a long one. While the rewards of fresh bread are amazing, behind every loaf are elements of time and process. Bread making ultimately begins with the sowing of grain into the ground. Long before the bread hits the shelf a farmer has gone out and plowed, sown the seed, watered, and harvested crops that form the basis of the

2. Jeffers, *The Greco-Roman World*, 20.

product. Sowing seed is the necessary precursor to baking bread. If there is no seed sown, there is no reward. It is this process of seed-sowing that Jesus picks up on in Mark 4. Using the image of the farmer disseminating seed Jesus taught:

> Listen! A farmer went out to sow his seed. As he was scattering the seed, some fell along the path, and the birds came and ate it up. Some fell on rocky places, where it did not have much soil. It sprang up quickly, because the soil was shallow. But when the sun came up, the plants were scorched, and they withered because they had no root. Other seed fell among thorns, which grew up and choked the plants, so that they did not bear grain. Still other seed fell on good soil. It came up, grew and produced a crop, some multiplying thirty, some sixty, some a hundred times. (Mark 4:3–8)

The image of a farmer sowing seed was familiar. The ancient farmer would go out into the field taking with him a bag of seed. Grabbing a handful of seed, the farmer would scatter it with the hope that the seed would take root in the ground and eventually grow to become a crop, hopefully "multiplying thirty, some sixty, some a hundred times" (4:8). The reality was, however, that there was no guarantee that the seed would find itself embedded in good soil. Jesus' further description of the process tells what happened to the seed sown by the farmer.

First, "some fell along the path, and the birds came and ate it up" (4:4). In Jesus' day there were not necessarily fenced areas separating properties. Often the defining boundary of someone's land was a path that people would walk on. It is upon this hardened dirt path that the first seed fell. The seed did not find root and was promptly snapped up by a hungry bird. Second, "some fell on rocky places" (4:5). Israel's rocky terrain meant that many fields sat on a shelf or thin layer of soil that would exist just above the rock. The seed, Jesus observed, germinates, but there is little room for roots. The growth is cut short, and the plant withers in death. Third, "other seed fell among thorns which grew up and choked the plants" (4:7). In the ancient world they didn't have insecticides. They would burn the fields in the hope of killing weeds, but inevitably weeds came back. The seed in this soil sprouts quickly, but is overtaken by the weeds that choke the life out of it. Finally, there is the seed that falls "on good soil. It came up, grew, and produced a crop, some multiplying thirty, some sixty, some a hundred times." This is the type of seed and soil mix every farmer hopes for. It is productive seed in productive soil. The net result is a bumper harvest, and with some more toil perhaps even fresh bread!

When Jesus told this story people were not perplexed with the issue of seed scattering. They understood it. They comprehended the process that the farmer followed and understood the natural progression of sowing and reaping. What they and the disciples missed, however, was what Jesus was illustrating through the parable. Fortunately, he explained this to his disciples in verses 14–20. This story, which is sometimes referred to as the "parable of the soils," was to illustrate the variety of responses that people have to God's word. Some reject it, some superficially accept it, some seem to receive it but then fall away, and finally some embrace God's word resulting in fruitfulness. Crucial to the whole process of the seed producing a crop, however, is "the farmer who sows the word" (4:14). For people to respond to God's word, it is necessary that they get the opportunity to hear it or read it. A farmer does not plant seed because he is bored; rather, a farmer plants seed in the anticipation that it will produce a crop.

In this parable we observe that the goal of sowing seed is fruitfulness. The person scatters the seed with the hope that it will produce. The believer who speaks God's truth is like the "farmer" who "sows the word" (4:15). The growth, as we will observe, is not dependent upon the farmer but on other external factors. The farmer's job, however, is to make sure the seed is sufficiently distributed and given its best chance to flourish. Paul saw himself as one of those whose job it was to scatter God's word. Writing to the Corinthian church he explained:

> *I planted the seed*, Apollos watered it, but God has been making it grow. So neither the one who plants nor the one who waters is anything, but only God, who makes things grow. The one who plants and the one who waters have one purpose, and they will each be rewarded according to their own labor. For we are co-workers in God's service; you are God's field. (1 Cor 3:6–9)

Paul's job as the farmer was to plant the seed of the word. Without planting the seed in the Corinthian church there would have been nothing to grow.

It is crucial in God's work that his word is proclaimed and his seed dispersed. For his word to bear fruit it must be given every opportunity to be disseminated because "faith comes from *hearing* the message, and the message is heard through the word about Christ" (Rom 10:17). The Christian, like a famer, needs to be in the seed-scattering business.

THE FARMER SOWS BUT EXPERIENCES MIXED RESULTS

Preaching is something that I have been doing for a little over twenty years. I am humbled by the weight and the privilege of having the opportunity to feed God's people through the explanation and application of the Scriptures. One of the things about preaching I sometimes find awkward, however, is the post-sermon response. The reason for this is because, after a sermon, people can sometimes be guilty of what a mentor of mine calls "the glorification of the worm" scenario. People file out of the church and, having heard God's word, they respond with a well-intentioned word of praise about the preacher as if the one delivering the message was the focus. Though there is an appropriateness to encouraging the one who has worked hard to teach God's word, the danger is that the preacher is tempted to believe that *they* are the source of the truth just proclaimed. The communicator of the word must keep perspective, however, by recognizing that they are simply the ones conveying the message; they are *not* the originator of it.

One of the most liberating things about the Christian message is that the success and power of God's word are utterly dependent upon him providing the blessing. The sower of seed had a responsibility of making sure the seed found its way into the ground, but there was no guarantee that it would produce a crop. His job was simply to cast the seed and trust that there would be growth. Jesus explained it this way to his disciples:

> A man scatters seed on the ground. Night and day, whether he sleeps or gets up, the seed sprouts and grows, though *he does not know how*. All by itself the soil produces grain—first the stalk, then the head, then the full kernel in the head. As soon as the grain is ripe, he puts the sickle to it, because the harvest has come." (Mark 4:26b–29)

The growth of the crop and its sprouting are not the work of a zealous farmer cheering on the seed. The growth of the kernel is not dependent on whether he is a rich farmer or a poor farmer. In fact the farmer, having planted the seed, "does not know how" it grows. The farmer just trusts that the soil will produce. Paul says that, like a farmer, he and Apollos were crucial in the planting and watering process, but it was God "who makes things grow" (1 Cor 3:7).

The Christian as Farmer

The Christian, like a farmer, scatters the seed but, just as the farmer does not always know whether the soil will be good or bad, so the Christian proclaims the word and trusts God to bring about growth. In Jesus' parable it is interesting that of the four different types of soil there is only one type that produces a long-lasting crop. The scattering process was the same for each soil, but only one produced a crop. As a seed sower of God's word it is not your job to bring people to conversion to Christ or to bring about their spiritual transformation. Your task, like the farmer, is simply to point people to God's word and have the confidence that it will not return to him empty. As the parable of the soils demonstrates, however, not every soil will be found to have produced fruits of righteousness. Offering a sobering assessment of judgment Paul offers caution when he exhorts the Galatians saying:

> Don't be misled—you cannot mock the justice of God. *You will always harvest what you plant.* Those who live only to satisfy their own sinful nature will harvest decay and death from that sinful nature. But those who live to please the Spirit will harvest everlasting life from the Spirit. (Gal 6:7–8, NLT)

On the last day Jesus, like a farmer, will separate the productive wheat from the destructive tares (Matt 13:24–30). As Jesus' hired hands, we are to sow the seeds of God's word and to leave the final judging of hearts to him. As Christians we sow the seed of God's word and trust him to do his work.

THE FARMER MUST BE WILLING TO WORK HARD

For a few of my teenage years our family lived on a kiwifruit orchard in New Zealand. Although I didn't appreciate the taste of kiwifruit at the time I became all too aware of the processes of planting, growing, and picking it. During one school year I picked up a temporary job as a "sorter" of kiwifruit. The process began with dozens of people picking the fruit from the vines and depositing them in large wooden crates. The fruit would then be unloaded on a conveyer belt where I, along with a dozen others, would "professionally" separate the fruit. If a fruit were too small, too large, the wrong color, or showing signs of age it would be put on one conveyer belt. If it were in good condition and fit for consumption it would be put on a separate conveyer belt where it would then be taken by a "handler" and placed into a prepared tray. The trays would then be moved to a special truck, and then taken to a distribution center where they would be further boxed in preparation for delivery to places like Tokyo, California, and London. Every time I now see a kiwifruit at the supermarket I'm reminded that the process of getting it on the shelf involves a whole journey of pickers, sorters, handlers, packers, and deliverers.

Being involved in the production process is hard work, but it has always been this way. Jesus uses the metaphoric language of production and the idea of hard work when talking about discipleship. When approached by a potential follower who stated, "I will follow you wherever you go" (Luke 9:57), Jesus responded by saying, "No one who puts a hand to the plow and looks back is fit for service in the kingdom of God" (Luke 9:62). Discipleship, like plowing a field, is serious business.

The proverbial statement about one who plows without looking back was commonly understood in Jesus' day. Hundreds of years earlier the Greek poet Hesiod spoke of the skillful person working the plow as "someone who puts care into his work and will drive a straight furrow, no longer gaping after his age-mates, but keeping his mind on his work."[3] Farming with a plow was a disciplined skill that required careful attention and focus. One writer explains:

> The very light Palestinian plough is guided with one hand. This one hand, generally the left, must at the same time keep the plough upright, regulate its depth by pressure, and lift it over the rocks and stones in its path. The ploughman uses the other hand to drive the unruly oxen with a goad about two yards long, fitted with an iron spike. At the same time he must continually look between the hindquarters of the oxen, keeping the furrow in sight. This primitive kind of plough needs dexterity and concentrated attention. If the ploughman looks round, the new furrow becomes crooked.[4]

By using the image of the cultivating famer Jesus was highlighting the difficulty of being his disciple. Just as plowing required a commitment and an attention to detail, so following Jesus required a wholehearted devotion to the task. The one tilling soil needed focus if they were to do the task correctly; any distractions would result in a crooked path, a lack of productivity, and time wasted. The follower of Christ, like the plowman, must keep the distractions of the world to a minimum and focus ahead on the

---

3. Hesiod, *Work and Days*, 442–43 (Best, trans.).
4. Jeremias, *Parables*, 195.

kingdom of God. There is no looking back in regret for the Christian, only looking onward and upward.

Jesus understood that this task of plowing was tough. After likening discipleship to plowing fields we read:

> Jesus appointed seventy-two others and sent them two by two ahead of him to every town and place where he was about to go. He told them, "The harvest is plentiful, but the workers are few. Ask the Lord of the harvest, therefore, to send out workers into his harvest field." (Luke 10:1–3)

In God's kingdom there is a shortage of gospel workers, they "are few." Christian service is counter-cultural and challenging. Few nowadays are willing to lift the plow of discipleship. Those who do are often distracted and end up plowing crooked paths. Few are those who endure to harvest time. Discipleship requires determination.

THE FARMER RECOGNIZES THE HARVEST

My favorite fruit of all time is definitely the mango. Mangoes, I believe, are one of God's best gifts to humanity! The only negative thing about mangoes is that their frequency as mangoes, like other fruits, is seasonal. So, unfortunately for me, mangoes are not around all year long. As different fruits ripen at various times of the year it is imperative that the farmer identifies when the season begins and when it ends. Harvest your crops too early and they will not reach maturity. Harvest them too late and they will begin to rot. It is critical that the farmers recognize and understand the right time to harvest.

Jesus understood not only the importance of sowing seed, he also understood the urgency of reaping at the right time. Having just sown the seed of the gospel in the heart of a Samaritan woman, Jesus taught his disciples that, just as there was a time for dispersing seed, there was also a time for reaping the results. To his disciples he said:

> Don't you have a saying, "It's still four months until harvest"? I tell you, open your eyes and look at the fields! *They are ripe for harvest.* Even now the one who reaps draws a wage and harvests a crop for eternal life, so that the sower and the reaper may be glad together. Thus the saying "One sows and another reaps" is true. I sent you to reap what you have not worked for. Others have done

the hard work, and you have reaped the benefits of their labor. (John 4:35–38)

Utilizing common wisdom about the time of harvest, Jesus informs his disciples as to the importance of gathering the harvest. As the Samaritans came out from the village Jesus indicated to his disciples that the seed he had planted in his conversation with a Samaritan woman was now leading to an opportunity for them to participate in the harvest of leading others to know God. With the villagers no doubt in mind, Jesus said, "open your eyes and look at the fields! They are ripe for the harvest" (4:35). Shortly after finishing this statement we read, "many of the Samaritans from the town believed in him because of the woman's testimony" (John 4:39). Though the disciples played no role in the seed-sowing, they did have the opportunity to reap a harvest of souls.

The fact that Jesus needed to tell his disciples to "open your eyes and look at the fields" indicates that they were somewhat unaware of what was in front of them. The Samaritans were ripe for a spiritual response and yet the disciples almost missed it. Lest we are too harsh with the disciples we must realize that we too have the same element of blindness. All around us there are people who are ripe to the Spirit's work. It could be the neighbors you've known for years but have never spoken with about Christ. It could be the classmate, or work colleague who has been watching your life but is too nervous to ask you about Christ. It could be a parent or sibling where God has been doing a work in their life and now all that is left is to give them the opportunity to respond. The challenge for you and me is whether we will join with the "Lord of the harvest" to reach them. The question is whether our eyes are open to the harvest in front of us?

WHAT CAN WE LEARN FROM THE FARMER?

The culture of Jesus' day was steeped in agriculture. Unlike our day where people esteem professions like lawyers and medical doctors, in the first-century world people revered the farmer. Without farmers you had very little to eat. Farmers needed to work the land, understand the seasons, and harvest at the right time in order to put food on the tables of the people. The hard work and skill of the farmer provide a wonderful backdrop to how we think about ourselves as Christians. There are many things that the ancient farmer can teach us, but four stand out.

GENEROUSLY SOW GOD'S WORD

To get a reasonably sized crop as a farmer meant that one must plant plenty of seed. As we've seen, not every soil is "good soil" and not every seed produces healthy plants and good crops. When the farmer casts the seed onto the ground he has no idea which will provide him with a crop, so in order to give himself the best chance of a return the farmer simply scatters as much seed as he has over a wide area. If the farmer sowed sparingly there would be less chance of a bountiful crop; the more he spreads the better the chance of genuine growth. What is true of the farmer is true of Christian ministry as well. Like farmers we are sowers. We, however, are not sowing physical seeds into the ground but spiritual seeds into the hearts of people. The crop we are interested in reaping is not a temporary seasonal one but a "crop for eternal life" (John 4:37).

One of the prime tasks of the believer is to scatter the seed of the gospel as far and as wide as we can. In order for God's word to take root in the lives of others we should, as much as we are able, get the truth out there. There are several ways that we can do this.

1. Share the Truths of the Gospel with Others

After leaving high school I completed an apprenticeship in the printing industry. My boss, at that time, was an old man named Bruce. Everyday I would arrive at work and be greeted by Bruce the same way. Bruce would say, "G'day champ! What do you know?" Though he wasn't really interested in whether I had some new inkling of knowledge I decided one day to respond to his question with a Bible verse. So I walked into work and Bruce asked me, "What do you know?" I responded with an answer, straight from the Gospel of Luke. I said, "Bruce, I know that the Son of Man came to seek and save the lost!" (Luke 19:10). The response was silence, then raucous laughter from my older colleague! From that day on, almost as if a game, Bruce would come out from his desk in the morning and, while gathered around the coffee machine with my workmates, ask the inevitable question, "Malcolm, what do you know?" Over the course of the next year or two my fellow workers became quite accustomed to, and amused by, my biblical responses. As a result they heard that I knew that:

> God so loved the world that he gave his one and only Son, that whoever believes in him shall not perish but have eternal life. (John 3:16)
>
> The wages of sin is death, but the gift of God is eternal life in Christ Jesus our Lord. (Romans 6:23)
>
> Here is a trustworthy saying that deserves full acceptance: Christ Jesus came into the world to save sinners—of whom I am the worst. (1 Tim 1:15)

Though at one level this was simply a bit of fun banter that I had with my boss, I believed it was so much more. On an almost daily basis I was presented with an opportunity to scatter God's word. Now I, until this day, have no idea whether it made an iota of difference in the lives of my colleagues, but I am confident that they heard the gospel on multiple occasions through simply exposing them to God's word.

Now my greeting approach may not be the way to go for you, but I think the seed-scattering principle is clearly one each of us should take seriously. You and I don't know how people will respond to the seed of God's word, but that ultimately is not our responsibility. I need to give the word of God the best chance to grow by getting it out there. To scatter seed we can read the Bible with others, whether Christian or not. We can incorporate what God is teaching us through his word in our everyday conversations. We can add to an email or a card a Bible verse. We ought to be as creative as we can in scattering God's word if we want to see productive fruit as the result.

2. Sow the Seeds of the Gospel through Giving

One of the ways that we can effectively scatter seed is through our financial giving. In 2 Corinthians 8–9 Paul appeals to a church to further the gospel work through sharing their monetary resources. Evidently there were some believers doing it tough and who were economically destitute, so in order to support them and to expand the work of God the Apostle Paul invited the Corinthians to join in the ministry of sowing seeds by financially contributing to those in need. He wrote, "whoever sows sparingly will also reap sparingly, and whoever sows generously will also reap generously" (2 Cor 9:6). Paul was not interested in fleecing the flock, as some now do, rather he was saying to the Corinthians that they could partner with other seed-sowing ministries with the very real benefit that one day they would reap a rich spiritual dividend.

As we financially contribute to the ministry we scatter seed as we empower others to serve. You may not be able to teach the Bible to Nepali people in Jiri. You may not be able to read the Bible with the tribal people of Peru. You may never have the chance to interact with a university student over the gospel, or speak to an inmate in prison. By financially supporting missionaries, churches, and para-church organizations, however, we can extend our reach with the gospel. While we may not see the fruit this side of heaven, we can be confident that "whoever sows generously will also reap generously."

TRUST GOD TO WORK THROUGH YOU

A few years ago the grandfather of a friend of mine was ill and dying. With the impending death of his grandfather my friend's extended family came to him as the "religious guy" looking for answers. As I spoke with my friend he explained how burdened he felt by the family because they were looking to him to make sure that their grandfather would be right with God when he died. My friend had spoken with his grandfather in the past but the elderly man had never embraced the gospel. My friend felt as if he had failed because his grandfather had not trusted in Christ. During our conversation I reminded him that converting someone to Christ was not his job. His job was simply to explain the gospel and trust God to do his sovereign work in the life of his grandfather. Whether the grandfather trusted Christ or not was not the responsibility of my friend, his job was simply to scatter seed. Did I want him to share Christ with his grandfather? Yes! Did I expect him to produce the spiritual rebirth of his grandfather? No. The liberating truth is that just as the farmer scatters seed and then depends on elements outside of himself for growth, so also the Christian shares God's message and then depends on God to produce lasting spiritual fruit.

As you and I scatter God's truth there will be times when it will feel fruitless. As mentioned earlier, I would quote Bible verses directly to my work colleagues as a young apprentice. I'd love to say that some of them came to Christ, or thought deeply about their relationship with God, but from my perspective I didn't see any obvious result from the seed I scattered. Was my work in vain? I don't think so because often God's best work is hidden from our sight.

While there are some among us who are seemingly gifted at reaping we must never think that a lack of visible response to our seed-sowing makes it useless. God is looking for faithful and generous sowers. Remember that God is the one who produces the fruit, not the sower or the reaper. One of the dangers of the contemporary church-planting movement is that often there is seemingly a great dependence on the "lead pastor" to produce numbers of converts to grow the church. The failure in this is that real growth is out of the hands of the pastor no matter how gifted they are. *God adds the growth, and that is why he, and he alone, should get all the glory when people respond to his word.*

The farmer sees that "the seed sprouts and grows, though *he does not know how*" (Mark 4:27). There are times when you and I will share God's word and it will be met with stiff resistance; at other times the very same words will have a deep life-changing impact on someone. What is the difference? The soil. Some people's hearts are receptive while others are hard. It is neither your job nor mine to work out which soil is which. Like farmers we must simply spread generously the seed of God's word and trust that God will do his work through it. When we discover it is about faithful seed-scattering and not dependent upon our ability to make the seeds grow, then we will feel the liberation that is found in trusting God.

WORK HARD FOR THE GOSPEL BY KEEPING YOUR FOCUS

The farming metaphor reminds us that being a disciple is hard work. Just as working the land to produce potatoes, corn, or wheat requires many hours and considerable sweat and endurance, so working in God's field as a disciple of Christ is hard going. Plowing was both physically and mentally demanding work. The successful famer concentrated on the task at hand and remained focused on his work. In the midst of plowing a field, however, the temptation for the farmer was to look back over their shoulder to view what had been worked. The distraction of looking back, however, would inevitably lead the person plowing to lose their way, as they would stray off course. In a similar manner, to be effective farmers in God's field we must be aware of our task and keep looking onward and upward.

One of the big dangers you and I face as Christians is to lose focus and in particular to become distracted by our past. I've met many Christians who, having followed Christ for many years, look back on their life before

Christ and, often in moments of discouragement, idealize the past that they have left behind. Sadly for some of these they have put down the plow and abandoned Christ in the futile hope that they will find peace and satisfaction. They seldom discover joy in their old ways.

There are times in our lives where we are tempted to give up and return to the state we were in before Christ saved us. We erroneously tend to think the grass is greener and the life easier in our former way. Maybe even as you read this you are tempted to let go of the plow and leave the task of discipleship. You may perhaps have even let go of the plow already. Fortunately our gracious and forgiving Master invites us time and time again to pick things up and keep plowing. The Apostle Paul understood the difficult of this discipleship plowing. Writing to the Galatian church, which had begun to lose its way, he wrote, "Let us not become weary in doing good, for at the proper time *we will reap a harvest* if we do not give up" (Gal 6:9).

The Scriptures remind us that, "we *will* reap a harvest if we do not give up." It doesn't say "you *may* reap a harvest" or "if you *are perfect* you will reap a harvest." God is simply looking for you and I to be faithful sowers. The faithful seed-sowing missionary who has served over many years with no apparent conversions will reap a harvest. The consistent Christian businessman who disperses God's word faithfully yet is met with antagonism and disdain will reap a harvest. The stay-at-home mother who patiently invests Christian wisdom in her children will reap a harvest. The key is faithfulness. Yes, it is hard being consistent as a disciple. Yes, it is discouraging when so many others leave the plow. Yes, it is tough when you don't always see growth. In spite of the challenges, however, we must faithfully keep our hands on the plow and trust that our obedience to Christ will be worth it. We must keep looking forward rather than looking back.

LOOK FOR OPPORTUNITIES TO REAP THE HARVEST

The farmer cultivates the harvest when it is ripe. If he doesn't reap the crop it will rot. With great urgency Jesus taught his disciples, and by extension us, that there are many people out there who are ripe for the spiritual harvest. In our midst there are those who are asking questions about the purpose of their existence and God is at work in their life and convicting them of their need of a savior. The problem we have, like the disciples, is that we are often too blind to observe the harvest.

Knowing Who You Are

It would be helpful if people walked around town with signs on their back that read "hard soil" or "good soil." The reality is, however, we don't know what God is doing in the lives of those around us. There are people in our neighborhoods, workplaces, schools, and families who are feeling lost and convicted. They need the Savior but often they are waiting to be introduced to him. They are ripe, but need harvesting.

Reaping calls for us to display elements of boldness and also urgency. We must be willing to open our eyes to the spiritual condition of those around us. The best way to gauge a person's spiritual condition, of course, is to talk plainly with them about the gospel.

One of my personality flaws is that I have a tendency to minimize conflict. If I'm at a restaurant and the meal is lousy I'm too polite to say anything lest I offend the waiter. If somebody makes a comment that I think is wrong or out of line I will normally suck it up and say nothing. I tend to live out the British mantra, "keep calm, and carry on." While some would say my conflict minimization is a good thing, in that I like to keep the peace, it can actually be a bit unhelpful at times, not the least in sharing the gospel. While I have no problem being a sower of seeds, the point of reaping is the place where I have often struggled. I have a fear that asking someone to come to Christ will rock the boat, wreck the relationship, and cause an awkward friction. I'm scared people will say "no" to the gospel.

I don't think I'm alone in my struggle with spiritual reaping. I think many of us mistakenly connect someone's response to the gospel as an indicator of whether they like us or not. We erroneously, at that point, place our personal value on the same level as the importance of sharing the gospel. What I've been learning over the last little season of life is that I must show my dependence, and trust that the one who will produce growth is capable of doing it. I have been reminding myself that whether someone responds negatively or positively toward the gospel is not dependent on my ability or connected to whether a person likes me or not. I need to demonstrate faith that God will act and if the answer is "no" to the gospel I am not to think that I have failed.

In recent times I've actually come to be surprised how receptive people actually are to the gospel if I will just open my mouth with the goal of reaping. The farming metaphor calls for us not only to sow seed, but also to be prepared to reap the crops. Reaping is not just the privilege of the gifted or the bubbly extrovert; it is the work of God through ordinary people. Look around, the farmer tells us, and see the fields white for harvest.

REFLECTIONS

1. Plowing God's field is hard work. Some among us lose focus and look back on the past as if there is hope there, but this is to lose our way. How can we remain focused on the task God has before us?
2. What are some ways that you are involved in scattering God's word? If none, what are some small but creative ways that you can begin disseminating the message of Jesus?
3. Share with someone how you've experienced God's word taking root in your life and changing you, or how you've witnessed God producing the fruit in the lives of others.
4. Write down the name of four people you would like to come to Christ. Pray that God would do his work in their lives. Be willing to reap by asking them about their relationship with Christ.

PRAYER

> God of all peoples,
>   Thank you for the goods news of your word that changes lives. We thank you that through your word and Holy Spirit you impart life to all who will listen and receive. Just as we have been recipients of your grace, aid us now in taking the life-transforming message of Jesus to all nations. We pray for those serving you in difficult parts of the world that you would allow them to see that their labor is not in vain. For those sharing in hostile and resistant countries encourage them to keep their hands to the plow. Raise up, Lord of the harvest, more workers for your fields. Help us to be willing to serve and to speak in whatever part of your world you place us. We trust you to produce good fruit that remains. Delight to use us as ambassadors who speak of your Son the Lord Jesus Christ.
>   Amen.

6

The Christian as Steward

"Each of you should use whatever gift you have received to serve others, as faithful stewards of God's grace in its various forms."

—1 Peter 4:10

"From everyone who has been given much, much will be demanded; and from the one who has been entrusted with much, much more will be asked."

—Luke 12:48

In my office sitting on the bookshelf is a cracked jar from the ancient city of Jericho. The aged vessel dates from around 1800–2000 BC and due to its many cracks it appears as old as its date. The jar itself was likely used to store olive oil and I've often wondered how, when, and by whom it was used. It was purchased through a renowned archeologist in Jerusalem and because it was acquired on my first trip to Israel it holds considerable sentimental value. My tiny clay olive jar takes pride of place in my office.

Every now and then, while teaching on biblical backgrounds, I will take the fractured jug to one of my lectures. Though it weighs very little, I'm always very interested in watching the students' responses as I invite them to pass it around. Some students love to touch and feel the coarse texture of the hardened clay. They fastidiously examine every curve and crack and take much care in their dealing with the ancient artifact. Others students, however, are reluctant to handle the jar and are happy to observe it from a distance. Because the vessel is several thousand years old they would rather refrain from touching it than to hold it with the fear of further damaging it.

Suppose one day I arrived to class intending to talk about cooking utensils in the ancient world and I then realized I had forgotten the jar in my office. Wanting to have the students physically assess the oil jar I then make a decision to have a student fetch the vessel. As the object is precious, somewhat delicate, and has personal value I look around the class and contemplate which student I should commission to get it. In making this decision there would be a few things I would want to consider. Is the student reliable and responsible? Does the student understand the value of the freight? Will the student handle the jar with care? Would the student treat the object as if it were theirs? As the owner of the prized item, I wouldn't just entrust this to anyone, I would seek to only employ someone trustworthy and reliable. What I would be after is what the ancient world called *"the steward."*

The English term "steward" is one that we rarely use in modern language. The name itself derives from the old English word *stigweard* coming from *stig* (house, hall) and *weard* (ward, keeper, guardian). The word "steward" and the related term "stewardship" are tied to the concept of the management, care, and responsible actions of one whose job it is to look after another's possessions or interests. In the ancient world the practice of employing someone to work as a "steward" was common. In one ancient letter, for example, we read of a landowner addressing his steward in regard to the management of his property. We read:

> I have empowered you by this document to administer my estate in Arsinoe, and to collect the rents and, if need be, to arrange new leases or to cultivate some land yourself, and to give receipts in my name, and to transact any business connected with stewardship, just as I transact it when I am present, and to distribute the plots in Karamis, restoring to me what remains over, as to which matter I rely on your good faith, and I confirm whatever you decided about them.[1]

In this example we can observe that people employed others to "steward" their property, financial investments, and the day-to-day running of their personal affairs. Stewardship like this was widely practiced across most cultures, and a familiar occupation to those living in Bible times.

---

1. BGU 1:300.

THE STEWARD IN THE ANCIENT WORLD

In the majority of ancient writings referring to the "steward" and "stewardship" the terms are strongly connected to a managerial and representative activity. The Greek historian Xenophon, for example, recorded that a steward was someone who was "put in charge of another man's estate."[2] He further explained that the steward "would get a good salary if, after taking over an estate, he continued to pay all outgoings, and to increase the estate by showing a balance."[3] The steward governed someone else's belongings and if done competently they could earn a healthy wage.

In other works we discover that "steward" was used of people managing everything from the family business to the kitchen in one's home. A steward's role in managing the day-to-day running of a household could include overseeing building campaigns. A steward could sometimes be placed in supervision over soldiers, and could even act as a type of judge in disputes.

Although in ancient Greece the term was usually contained to the role of governing a home, with the arrival of the Roman Empire the term took on an even more expansive idea and came to represent "all sorts of managers in the civil realm."[4] By the time of the New Testament there were large numbers of stewards in government, city administration, guilds, and even religious societies. One writer concludes, "the number of 'stewards' in the service of local authorities, the province, or the empire for keeping records, collecting taxes, or carrying out day-to-day administrative matters was staggering."[5]

In the ancient world the steward, whether commissioned to oversee an estate or act in a civic role, was given responsibility and ultimately held accountable for their actions. In the larger community the "steward" was viewed as a person of esteem and importance because their duty was a visible demonstration that someone in higher authority had considered them trustworthy.

---

2. Xenophon, *Economics*, 1.2 (Marchant, trans.).
3. Ibid., 1.4.
4. Reumann, *Stewardship*, 13.
5. Ibid. 13–14.

THE STEWARD IN THE OLD TESTAMENT

Given the familiarity of stewards and stewardship in the ancient world it should not surprise us to discover the term and the practice in the pages of Scripture. Most of the accounts using the term "steward" reflect ideas of management and responsibility.

In Genesis, for example, we read that Joseph engaged the aid of "the *steward* of his house" (43:16). In this context, Joseph was serving in the capacity of a ruler and employed the "steward" as one who would act on his behalf. That the steward carried an element of representation of his master can be seen in the manner in which the brothers of Joseph addressed the steward. When speaking to him they began with, "we beg your pardon, *our lord*" (Gen 43:20). Though the steward was a servant of Joseph, he was treated with the respect that one would grant to a superior. The steward's position of authority was clearly connected with his relationship to his master.

In the Joseph story we also see that a steward was given the responsibility to execute the desires of his master. Joseph commanded his steward to perform certain tasks (Gen 44:1) and the steward obediently fulfilled them (Gen 44:6). In this manner the steward made decisions not based upon his own initiative, but simply executed the commands of his master. In this regard the steward acted as the trusted servant of the one he worked for. Hall explains:

> The steward in the literature of the Old Testament is a servant, but not an ordinary servant who simply takes orders and does the bidding of others. Rather he . . . is a rather superior servant, a sort of supervisor or foreman, who must make decisions, give orders, and take charge . . . That is, the steward is one who has been given the responsibility for the management and service of something belonging to another, and his office presupposes a particular kind of trust on the part of the master.[6]

While the steward in Genesis is seen to be obedient and loyal to his superior, we discover that not all were. In Isaiah 22:15–19, for example, we have a strong condemnation of a wayward steward. It reads:

> Go, say to this *steward*,
> to Shebna the palace administrator:

---

6. Hall, *The Steward*, 32.

> What are you doing here and who gave you permission
> > to cut out a grave for yourself here,
> hewing your grave on the height
> > and chiseling your resting place in the rock?
>
> "Beware, the Lord is about to take firm hold of you
> > and hurl you away, you mighty man.
> He will roll you up tightly like a ball
> > and throw you into a large country.
> There you will die
> > and there the chariots you were so proud of
> > will become a disgrace to your master's house.
> I will depose you from your office,
> > and you will be ousted from your position."

In this example the steward clearly had lost perspective as to his relationship with the master. While it was possible for a steward to act without consulting their master, the independence condemned in this passage seems to have been based on the fact that Shebna's actions were presumptuous and not in the best interests of his superior. The net result of Shebna's poor stewardship was that he was removed from his position of responsibility (Isa 22:19). From this judgment we can observe that, while the steward was a valued servant who had a duty to fulfill, they were also held accountable for their actions.

THE STEWARD IN THE NEW TESTAMENT

As mentioned earlier, by the time of the New Testament the concept of stewardship had broadened from household responsibilities to be a term that could indicate civic leadership. While there are references to officials acting in a stewardship capacity, such as Erastus (Rom 16:23), the New Testament's interest is not so much in the office of the steward but rather what the role can teach us. The practice of stewardship is used, particularly in Jesus' teaching, as an illustration to shape how the Christian should think about their identity. In particular, there are two aspects of stewardship that the believer in Christ should reflect on: namely, the steward is one given responsibility, and is one who will also be held accountable.

The Steward Is Responsible

First, we find that Jesus uses the role of the steward in order to communicate how each believer is given an element of responsibility. In Luke 12 Jesus likens believers to stewards in the midst of his teaching about financial prosperity. In this chapter, he addresses the inheritance of material wealth (12:13–15), the danger of coveting another's possessions (12:16–21), worrying too much about personal comfort (12:22–34), and finally how the disciple should view physical assets in light of the future judgment (12:35–40). To illustrate his teaching Jesus then tells a story of a "manager," that is a steward, as an image to help us understand how believers should live as Jesus' followers. Jesus taught:

> Who then is the faithful and wise manager, whom the master puts in charge of his servants to give them their food allowance at the proper time? It will be good for that servant whom the master finds doing so when he returns. Truly I tell you, he will put him in charge of all his possessions. But suppose the servant says to himself, "My master is taking a long time in coming," and he then begins to beat the other servants, both men and women, and to eat and drink and get drunk. The master of that servant will come on a day when he does not expect him and at an hour he is not aware of. He will cut him to pieces and assign him a place with the unbelievers.
> The servant who knows the master's will and does not get ready or does not do what the master wants will be beaten with many blows. But the one who does not know and does things deserving punishment will be beaten with few blows. From everyone who has been given much, much will be demanded; and from the one who has been entrusted with much, much more will be asked. (Luke 12:42–48)

What Jesus demonstrates in this parable is that there are basically two types of steward. First, there is the "faithful and wise manager" (12:42), and second is the steward who "does not do what the master wants" (12:47). Obviously Jesus desires that his followers would emulate the mindset of the first type of steward. As is clear from the context, Jesus is teaching his disciples, and by extension us, that when it comes to thinking about our material possessions we should frame the way we think about it in regard to how a "faithful and wise" steward would think about diligently governing a house.

Knowing Who You Are

The first thing we notice about the steward is that their work involves the distribution of things that are *not* their own. The "*master* puts in charge" (12:42) and the stewards are "*given* much" (12:48). The stewards are granted responsibility, but what they have they can't claim ultimate ownership of, as they have been "*entrusted*" (12:48) with it. They are managers, that is to say stewards, *not* owners.

By nature we like to possess things. It has been said of children that when they are learning to speak there is one word that they acquire without any instruction, "mine." As parents, Tamara and I have observed that our children are quick to receive gifts, but often slow to respond with "thank you." Our children, and I'm sure they're not alone in this, often fail to appropriately recognize the generosity of the one giving them the presents. They presumptuously take the gifts as if it were their right or privilege rather than understanding it as an act of benevolence from a generous giver. The self-centered nature evidenced in most children continues to adulthood and reflects the natural disposition of all of us, particularly as it relates to God's generosity toward us.

In God's economy he gives gracious gifts to his children. He furnishes some people with outstanding intellects, some with skills in working with people, others with careers in teaching, medicine, or counseling. He gives us occupations that allow us to earn income, which in turn provides us with new cars, enjoyable holidays, and comfortable houses. The temptation we face, however, like the child with the gift, is to think that what we have is *our entitlement* and in doing so we can forget that we are not originators of the gifts we have, but stewards of them. The steward is "given" and "entrusted" with responsibility. He or she is a steward, *not* the owner of the things given to them.

Second, we notice in Jesus' parable that the steward is given a task with the expectation that they will accomplish it. We read that the steward's responsibility was to oversee the household servants and "to give them their food allowance at the proper time" (Luke 12:42). It is clear from the comment—"my master is taking a *long* time in coming"—that the master leaves the entrusted steward (12:45). As with examples from both the Old Testament and other parts of the ancient world we see that the steward could, and often did, act independently of the master. Whether the master was there or not, however, the expectation was that the steward would wisely use the resources he had been granted for the benefit of the master.

In a similar parable to the one found in Luke, Matthew 25:14–30 records the story of three stewards who were each given bags of gold by a master who then went away. When the master returned clearly his expectation was that the trusted stewards had all used the gold wisely. While two of them were industrious and made the most of that which they were given, one did nothing with the wealth. The response of the master to the idle steward was one of anger, "you wicked, lazy servant!" (Matt 25:26). The master distributed his belongings to his stewards with the clear expectation that they would use them profitably.

The Steward Is Accountable

A second observation we can make in regard to the teaching of the New Testament about stewardship relates to the issue of accountability. Both of the steward parables in Luke 12 and Matthew 25 are significantly couched in teaching associated with the return of Jesus on the last day. This is significant because as Jesus spoke to his disciples about using their God-given resources he was also reminding them of the expectation that he would return and there would be a subsequent examination of how the entrusted gifts were used. The stewards, as we see in the respective parables, were to perform their duties while keeping in mind that the master would one day return and ask them to provide an account. We see two responses. The one who was "faithful and wise" (Luke 12:42) and addressed as the "good and faithful servant" (Matt 25:21) was the one who worked hard, invested wisely, and yielded growth for the master. This one is praised and given further responsibility as a result of his obedience (Luke 12:44).

The wicked and unfruitful steward, in contrast, is the one who lived as though the master was not returning. This steward spent his time carelessly eating, drinking, and getting drunk. He did nothing with the master's wealth, instead chose to live for the moment with no obvious concern about furthering the interests of the master. In the case of the "lazy steward" in Matt 25:26 it was not even an issue of abusing the gifts that were given by the master, but just the neglect in not even using them at all that brought about this steward's scathing condemnation.

A steward was entrusted with the wealth of the master and expected to use this for the benefit of his superior. Apathetic indifference and inaction would result in harsh judgment. To fail to live in light of the return of the master was extremely unwise. On the other hand, using the master's gifts and resources shrewdly would result in blessing. The steward who demonstrated responsibility would receive favor and further responsibility from the master.

What is overwhelmingly clear from the teachings of Jesus is the fact that whether the outcome is positive or negative the steward *will* be judged. Concluding his parable Jesus solemnly warns, "from everyone who has been given much, much will be demanded; and from the one who has been entrusted with much, much more will be asked" (Luke 12:48). The steward will be held to account.

WHAT CAN WE LEARN FROM THE STEWARD?

Over the last decade many of the great superheroes of my childhood have managed to make their way back to the big screen. Movies like *Batman*, *The Incredible Hulk*, and *X-Men* have brought new life to legendary characters of yesteryear. One of my favorites has to be Spiderman. Evidently I'm not the only person who thinks the sleek superhero in the red mask is awesome as the combined income of the recent Spiderman movies exceeded $2.5 billion, making it the tenth top grossing franchise of movies of all time.

The basic storyline of Spiderman revolves around a young man named Peter Parker who, through circumstances beyond his control, ends up inheriting the superpowers of having spiderlike agility and web-making skills. The movies revolve around the life of Peter as he wrestles with the tensions of being a normal kid, on the one hand, and a superhero on the other. Summing up his predicament in life is a statement made in the movie by his Uncle Ben, "With great power comes great responsibility."

The origin of this now world-famous statement—"with great power comes great responsibility"—has been the subject of much debate. Search the internet and you will find this quote attributed to the writer of Spiderman, Stan Lee, along with others including Franklin D. Roosevelt and Winston Churchill, while some even suggest Voltaire made the original statement, in French no less. At the end of the day, however, the idea behind this catchy maxim is nothing new. The concept picked up in the Spiderman adage is one that is exemplified in the ancient function of the steward. A steward was one who had been granted responsibility by a superior master, and because of this responsibility came the expectation they would respond with appropriate diligence. To change Spiderman's line we might say that for the ancient steward, "with much responsibility comes equal accountability."

Whoever coined the now famous Spiderman phrase, whether knowingly or not, was merely echoing Jesus' statement in Luke 12:48: "from everyone who has been given much, much will be demanded." We all understand that responsibility carries great weight. For the Christian, however, the stewardship theme provides an important reminder of both our commitment to Christ as well as our accountability to him. With this in mind, what are some things we can learn from the "steward" imagery used of the Christian? Four implications stand out.

1. Recognize What God Has Given You to Steward

I have many great memories of growing up in a terrific Sunday School at church. My dad would pick up local kids in a bus and we would all ride together to our little coastal church. While I can't tell you much about the structure of the services back then or the quality of preaching, I still remember several songs that we used to sing. One of them had this simple, but helpful chorus:

> Count your blessings, name them one by one.
> Count your blessings, see what God has done.
> Count your blessings, name them one by one.
> And it will surprise you what the Lord has done.

The basic premise of the refrain is that in our lives there are "blessings" to count. In fact, as this song correctly suggests, the number of them is for most of us a "surprise." God has providentially favored us with many gifts, and yet so often in life we fail to recognize just how much we have. The constant bombardment of the media deceives us into thinking that we are in need of *more* things, such as a new car, a slimmer body, and a better TV. The reality is, however, we have far more than we ever need. Yet most of us have not recently counted our blessings.

The Bible is clear that it is God who gives good gifts to his children. James 1:17 says, "*Every* good gift and every perfect gift is from above, *coming down from the Father of lights* with whom there is no variation or shadow due to change." The home you live in, the education you have received, the children you are raising, the ability to read, to work with your hands, to relate to people, to work as a schoolteacher, or as an actuary, or a bricklayer, have all been granted to you from the "Father of lights" who has created you.

God has wired and created you and me uniquely, and he has done so because he wants to use us for *his* greater purposes. As you read this you may be thinking, "God can't use me." It is easy for us to look around and see others who appear to be more gifted than we are and conclude that we are of little value. There is always someone with a better singing voice, a sharper intellect, and better people skills, and someone who may have even funnier jokes than we do. The reality is, however, God has not wired you to be them. God has created *you* to be *you*.

Jesus' parable of the talents in Matthew 25 indicates that not everybody was given the same amount of wealth. One of the stewards was given five bags of gold, another three bags, another one bag. It didn't make any difference as to whether one had five bags or one; it was still the master's property. God gives some of us five bags of responsibility and to others of us he gives one bag. What is true, however, is that God gives us only what he wants us to be responsible for.

God wants you to manage and steward what he has given you. Consider the family for example. God has given to Tamara and I three children. Like most parents we are proud of our kids and love them. Like most parents, however, we also struggle at times with their behavior. In moments when I'm tempted to get tetchy with my children, whether it's for fighting with each other, not cleaning their rooms, or even being defiant, rather than a fit of anger I try to remind myself that God, in his wisdom, chose to give Tamara and myself the task of raising *these* children. God sovereignly appointed us as stewards of these three small lives. At the point of my frustration I try to ask myself, "how can I shepherd my children now so that they will respond in a way that will help them understand who God is, and who he wants them to be?" In essence, I'm wanting to be a "wise and faithful steward" as I manage the children God has entrusted to me.

Now I recognize you may be reading this and may not have children, or your children are now older, but my point is simple. Whatever relationships God gives us, whether as a spouse, or an employee, or a Sunday school teacher, he does so for a purpose. He grants us responsibility with the desire that we will take what he gives us and use it for his glory. If God has blessed you with a large home, use it responsibly by sharing it with others. Open your house to missionaries, to singles, to families, to visitors, to Bible study groups. Steward your home. If God has blessed you with the job of being a physician, see your occupation not as a forty-hour per week "necessary evil" but a sacred opportunity to help people and demonstrate the love of God.

2. Faithfully Steward Your Gifts

The type of steward that Jesus praised was one that was first of all "faithful." In the ancient practice of stewardship the reliability factor of your employee was very important. To entrust your house, or gold, or business to someone meant that you had to believe that they would take the task seriously. In the Matthew 25 parable the master wasn't distressed that the man who was given two bags of gold didn't make as much profit as the one who was given five bags of gold. The master was most pleased that the stewards used what they were given to benefit his estate. The master was looking for a *faithful* and *trustworthy* steward.

As previously mentioned we are not all given the same types of personalities, careers, or families. We are wired uniquely to serve God in our own responsible way. The diversity of our stewardship can be seen in the words from 1 Peter 4:10–11 where the Apostle wrote:

> As each has received a gift, use it to serve one another, as *good stewards* of God's varied grace: whoever speaks, as one who speaks oracles of God; whoever serves, as one who serves by the strength that God supplies—in order that in everything God may be glorified through Jesus Christ.

God does not give us all the same gifts to steward. There are some who speak, some who serve, in fact there are a variety of ways. What God then is looking for in us is not for all of us to do the same things; rather, he is looking for whether we have been faithful over the long haul in using our unique responsibilities "in order that in everything God may be glorified through Jesus Christ" (1 Pet 4:11). Faithfulness does not equal being spectacular. Faithfulness means serving consistently with a deep commitment to the Master's bigger plan.

The "lazy" steward in Jesus' parable was condemned not for his misuse of what was entrusted to him. Rather, he was "lazy" because he failed to recognize the significance of the opportunity the master had given him. However God has wired you, and whatever life situation he has put you in, count your blessings and reflect on what opportunities he has given you to serve him. You will not be held accountable for how God has gifted your neighbor or your friend. You will be required to give an account of how *you* used the gifts that God has uniquely entrusted to you.

In the day-to-day running of our lives there are actually few moments when we *feel* like we are doing something useful for God. As somebody in vocational Christian work I would like to say that regularly I have spectacular moments of insight into God's word, or I see the lives of people change dramatically as they hear the word of God. In reality, however, my Christian ministry is not about numbers, or books, or blogs; it is about whether I'm persisting doing my Master's business. It's about faithfulness.

Edward Kimball was a steward of God who understood the significance of faithfulness. Living during the 1800s, Kimball was a humble man who faithfully plodded along in life serving God in his own sphere. One of the areas Kimball felt responsible for was the children in his Sunday School class at church. Kimball felt that as part of his stewardship he needed to share the gospel personally with each member of his Sunday School class.

One day Kimball went to a small shoe store where he met with a young seventeen-year-old boy who was a member of his class. With great anxiousness Kimball bumbled his way through the gospel and eventually led the young man to trust in Jesus. The young man was D.L. Moody who would go on to speak to thousands all over the world about the gospel. Years later as D.L. Moody preached a young man named Mordecai Ham committed to taking God's word seriously. He later went on to preach the good news message to which a young man named Billy Graham would respond. Billy Graham would become a great evangelist and ended up preaching the gospel all over the world including New Zealand, where a young boy named Graham Ashby would respond to the call of God. Years later Graham Ashby would serve as evangelist and would preach at a youth conference where I would respond to the gospel as a teenager. My trusting Christ was itself, in some form, the extension of the ministry of one humble man named Edward Kimball. Kimball had no idea about the significance of the fruit of his ministry yet I thank God that the unknown Edward Kimball took his stewardship seriously and was faithful in executing the humble task God gave him.

You and I don't know this side of eternity what difference our stewardship will make in the plans of God. We might not *feel* our gifts are as obvious or as significant as others, but this is not what pleases the Master. The Lord is looking for *faithfulness*. He desires that you and I simply and consistently exercise the gifts that he has given to us to make him known. We must faithfully steward our gifts.

3. Wisely Steward God's Money

Normally when most people hear the word "steward" in church they get nervous about money. In fact I have no doubt that some, maybe even you, had a reluctance to read this chapter because you knew the issue of personal finances would come up. Well, I'm glad you're still reading. The issue of stewardship is certainly much bigger than just one area of life. Having said that, one area that concretely reveals our understanding of stewardship is how we use our financial wealth.

The joke is sometimes made that several dollars were once having a conversation in someone's wallet. The $50 bill proudly boasted of the places it had been. "I've been in the care of celebrities, visited great restaurants as well at hotels." To this the $20 note commented, "I too have visited some great places and been in the hands of well known people." Finally the $1 chimed in, "all I've ever seen is church, church, church!" While we might laugh, or groan, at this, unfortunately there is an element of truth to the fact that for many giving money is not really a significant part of their Christian life.

One of the wrong ways we often frame giving in the church is by asking the question "how much shall I give?" When we reflect on the parable in Matthew 25 we notice in that story that the issue is not the *quantity*, as not everyone has the same numbers of bags of gold. The master didn't give them all five bags, or all one. He gave a variety. His expectation, however, was that they would use whatever the number of resources given to multiply his estate. In the parable the money is, every bag of it, the master's! When we ask, "what *percentage* of money should we give?" we are starting with the erroneous presumption that the money is all ours, yet it is not! The master owns it *all*. The master may give you a "bag of gold" type salary of two thousand, twenty thousand, or even two hundred thousand dollars a year. What you and I need to remember is that it *all* belongs to *him*! He provided you with the mind, the skills, and the education for you to earn money. So rather than viewing the income as yours, think about it as a bag of gold to invest for the Master.

The issue of giving is not "should I give God ten or twenty percent?" the issue is "how can I wisely steward the money God has given me?" There is great danger in thinking that money is ours and we can give God a portion. It's all his to begin with. As such we should think about how to best distribute what God gives us. This will look different for all of us. What should shape our common financial stewardship, however, is our commitment to enhancing the Master's work. In light of this Jesus offers us a timely reminder:

> Do not store up for yourselves treasures on earth, where moths and vermin destroy, and where thieves break in and steal. But store up for yourselves treasures in heaven, where moths and vermin do not destroy, and where thieves do not break in and steal. *For where your treasure is, there your heart will be also* . . . No one can serve two masters. Either you will hate the one and love the other, or you will be devoted to the one and despise the other. You cannot serve both God and money. (Matt 6:19–21, 24)

How we use our money is a good indicator of where our heart is as stewards. We are to be people who give generously "not reluctantly or under compulsion, for God loves a cheerful giver" (2 Cor 9:7). The master has *given* us "surpassing grace" in his "indescribable gift" (2 Cor 9:14) of Jesus. If the Master has shown such generosity and liberty in giving his gift, the implication is that his steward should wisely do the same. Wisely steward God's money.

4. Faithfully Steward the Gospel

Keeping the big picture is important for the one managing God's resources. Stewardship, as we've observed, involves the steward faithfully serving their master with an awareness of the fact that one day their labor will be assessed. The steward needs to keep focus on the big task. In a world that encourages us to climb to the top, enhance our reputation, become "someone," to keep the mindset of a humble steward is challenging. It is difficult, but not new. Paul was a man who had gained some traction as a preacher and as an apostle of Christ, yet he recognized that his gifting and service were simply the result of being appointed by his master. Writing to combat factional groups within the church he provided a self-description that was apt for himself, his followers, and also for us. He wrote, "This is how one should regard us, as servants of Christ and *stewards of the mysteries of God. Moreover, it is required of stewards that they be found faithful*" (1 Cor 4:1–2, ESV).

The Christian as Steward

The Christian is a steward for the Master and the nature of their stewardship is over "the mysteries of God" (4:1). As followers of Jesus we are granted the great responsibility of passing to others the wonderful mystery of God that is salvation found in Jesus Christ. We are not originators of God's message, but we are called to be responsible stewards who deliver the message to the world. Paul did not see himself as a famous celebrity, but a humble steward.

The announcement of the good news has been "entrusted" to the Christian steward. This message is to be faithfully delivered to others. As stewards we must "contend for the faith that was once for all *entrusted* to God's holy people" (Jude 3). Our responsibility is not to come up with the message, but simply to pass it on. Contending for the gospel is often difficult as family and friends can reject or ostracize us because of the message. In spite of this, however, we must remain faithful because "it is required of stewards that they be found faithful."

When I was a young boy one of my favorite games to play at birthday parties was "pass the parcel." A straightforward game, children pass a wrapped gift around a circle until the playing music stops. When the music ends the child with the parcel vigorously tears off a layer of wrapping and thus receives a small gift. Now that I have children of my own it is interesting to watch the dynamics of the game. When the children are small they innocently and joyfully "pass the parcel" around the circle. They are happy to share it with others and are pleased when others take joy of opening a layer. There comes a time, however, when the child turns about five or six years old and they realize how the game really works. At this age it becomes noticeable that rather than passing the parcel to others, they are more interested in holding onto the gift. As the music plays they tightly clutch the gift and very reluctantly pass it on. Their selfish nature begins to blossom as they seek to hold on to the gift.

As believers we can often behave like a child in "pass the parcel." God grants us all gifts and he does so very generously. With the provision God gives us, however, comes an assumed responsibility that we will steward what he gives us. God gives us good minds, education, health, relationships, homes, money, and many other gifts not so that we can live for ourselves, but that we might responsibly be distributors and multipliers of his generosity. Indeed, the good news message of the gospel is not simply a truth that we revel in, but a message of grace that we must handover to others. Rather than holding onto the parcel of God's good gifts, we must

Knowing Who You Are

graciously distribute them. Stewardship is the call to hold things loosely, use things wisely, and to live faithfully. We do this in anticipation of our Master's soon return.

REFLECTIONS

1. What stands out to you about the "steward" image in regard to your relationship with God and his people? What did you learn or were most challenged to remember in this chapter regarding stewardship?
2. What are the gifts that God has entrusted uniquely to you? Take time to recount your blessings, and as the song says, "name them one by one." Give thanks to God for these gifts.
3. Finish this statement. "Lord help me to be generous with your gifts by . . ."
4. Do an analysis of your yearly spending. In what ways could you be a better steward of the financial resources God has given you? Take time to come up with a planned commitment on how you will invest your Master's money.

PRAYER

> Generous gift-giving God,
> We thank you for the privileged position we have of being your stewards. You have gifted us with a variety of resources, skills, and experience. We acknowledge that every good thing we have comes from you. As we distribute, use, and manage the areas you have entrusted to us, help us to be both wise and faithful as we minister through your strength for your purposes. Grant us insight on how best to bless others as we seek to mirror your grace and generosity. Forgive us for holding too tightly to the gifts while forgetting about you the giver. Until your return empower us to serve you for Christ's sake.
> Amen.

7

The Christian as Soldier

> "Fight the good fight of faith."
> —1 Timothy 6:12

> "Ask yourself voluntarily which you would choose if some god gave you the choice—life in a café or life in a camp?"
> —Seneca, ca. 65 AD

> "Onward, Christian soldiers, marching as to war,
> With the cross of Jesus going on before.
> Christ, the royal Master, leads against the foe;
> Forward into battle see His banners go!"
> —Sabine Baring-Gould, 1869

ONE OF THE DELIGHTS that my wife, Tamara, and I have enjoyed over the last decade has been the privilege of regular Bible reading with our children. In our home we have, in a variety of formats, spent time with our kids both individually and collectively working through the Scriptures. Over the course of several years we have made our way through numerous children friendly editions of the Bible. One of the particularly fun things about reading the Bible with the kids is that they, along with us, enjoy seeing some of the artistic renditions of various biblical accounts. Whereas in my childhood only the *Good News* version of the Bible had drawings, most children's Bibles today have visuals to keep the reader engaged.

A little while ago while reading Revelation with my son I noticed a rather amusing drawing in one of his Bibles for children. The Apostle John, who is recorded in the book as being an exile on the island of Patmos, is pictured lying comfortably under a coconut tree on a white sandy beach with his hands behind his head, enjoying the sun while receiving his divine revelation of Jesus' glory. While the picture is colorful and engaging, John's experience was almost the complete opposite of what is presented. The island of Patmos was, and still is, a remote and very quiet island in the Aegean Sea. Rather than spending his days lounging about under coconut palms, John lived out his days slaving away in the mines as a prisoner on the island. He was not on a holiday, but was suffering hardship for the sake of the gospel.

Now, I don't want to be too harsh on the artist of the children's Bible as the cartoon-type drawings are really just designed to help the young readers remain engaged with the Bible. What I find telling in the artist's rendition of the Revelation account of John, however, is that the presentation of the apostle on Patmos is actually indicative of many people's understanding of the Christian life. For many out there, being a follower of Jesus, or a "Christian," means living a rewarding, comfortable, and personally fulfilling life. Those following this line of thought suggest that because we have been born-again our current experience should be one of "victory" as we live the life we've always desired. The Christian life, it is reasoned, should be a wonderfully harmonious and satisfying experience, as opposed to the purposeless existence of being without Christ.

While there is an element of truth in that God desires that we live a full and purposeful life, there is very little in Scripture to suggest that this means God's intention for us is that we live in an extended season of wealth and pain-free bliss in our current broken world. In fact, the evidence is overwhelmingly the opposite, in that the Christian life here and now is presented in the Scriptures as one filled with challenges and even hardship. Numerous times throughout the Scriptures the believer is pictured as one striving in a combat, a conflict, a fight. The apostle Paul writes:

> For we do not *wrestle* against flesh and blood, but against the rulers, against the authorities, against the cosmic powers over this present darkness, against the spiritual forces of evil in the heavenly places. (Eph 6:12)

The Christian as Soldier

In this instance, the image Paul uses is one of the Christian lifestyle as a "wrestle," that is to say a struggle, a spiritual battle, a warring contest. He acknowledges that the tensions we face as believers are real and difficult. Herein lies the constant friction of the Christian experience. Though we acknowledge that Jesus is the king, we currently live in a broken world that refuses to bow to his authority. We reside in a world where it seems evil people *do* prosper, injustice *does* abound, and death and decay regularly dominate our lives. So how do we remain godly in a godless world as we wait for Jesus to return and make all things new? The answer, at least in part, lies in another New Testament image, that of the Christian as soldier.

THE SOLDIER AND WAR IN THE ANCIENT WORLD

War is nothing new. Since the dawn of time there have always been conflicts. Some wars have been fought over ideologies and religion, others over land, and still others have been waged out of revenge for sins committed in the past. Whatever the case, war has touched virtually every culture in every time period of history in some form or another.

In the ancient world war was a regular part of life. Kingdoms rose and just as quickly fell. Famous rulers like Cyrus, Alexander the Great, and Julius Caesar were best known not for the peace they provided during their day as much as their military conquests. Statues, busts, and monuments littered the ancient world with tales of battles and bloodshed. People warred against each other and, while there were seasons of peace, the masses knew that the next war was never far away.

Due to the prevalence of war most were familiar with military obligation and the role of the soldier in the battle. In a formal process known as the *sacramentum militiae* men would become soldiers by swearing an oath indicating their allegiance to the emperor and his empire.[1] Such a commitment signified their willingness to commit to battle and that they would "not abandon their ranks for flight or fear."[2] Such soldiers were a necessary part of society and their obedience and commitment to their respective king or emperor were to serve as a model for the rest of the community.

Over time the character traits of the soldier became something to be considered worthy of imitation in life. Writing to his friend Lucilius, the

---

1. See Polybius, *Histories*, 6.21.1–4. In the ancient world very few women were permitted to be soldiers.

2. Livy, *Histories of Rome*, 22.38.4 (Foster, trans.).

Knowing Who You Are

Roman statesman Seneca uses the soldier as a metaphor of the courageous person who takes risks and works hard, unlike the ignoble rich person who rests on their laurels. He wrote:

> And yet *life*, Lucilius, *is really* a *battle*. For this reason those who are tossed about at sea, who proceed uphill and downhill over toilsome crags and heights, who go on campaigns that bring the greatest danger, are heroes and front-rank fighters; but persons who live in rotten luxury and ease while others toil, are mere turtle-doves—safe only because men despise them.[3]

Rather than living the easy life, Seneca challenged his friend to be like "front-rank fighters" and to respond to the trials of life like a soldier would a war, not like "turtle-doves."

To soldier through life meant to live with discipline, focus, and obedience. Calling on his friend to submit to the trials of his life and to persevere like a good soldier Seneca further advised:

> Whatever happens, assume that it was bound to have happened, and do not be willing to rail at Nature. That which you cannot reform, it is best to endure, and to attend uncomplainingly upon the god under whose guidance everything progresses; for it is a bad *soldier* who grumbles when following his commander. For this reason we should welcome our orders with energy and vigor, nor should we cease to follow the natural course of this most beautiful universe, into which all our future sufferings are woven.[4]

For Seneca, rather than looking at the downside of life he suggested to his reader that he should "welcome" his "orders with energy and vigor." Elsewhere he concludes his thoughts on the battle of life with the challenge:

> Ask yourself voluntarily which you would choose if some god gave you the choice—life in a café or life in a camp?[5]

Clearly for Seneca being a good soldier in life meant making sacrifices. It was not the life of ease in the café but the gritty hardship of life with the troop in the camp.

Living the life of a soldier was clearly not a light decision. Another Stoic philosopher, Epictetus, who also likened life to a type of battle, wrote

---

3. Seneca, *Moral Epistles*, 96.5 (Gummer, trans.).
4. Ibid., 107.9.
5. Ibid.,,96.5.

of the complexity of choosing the soldier-type approach to life's difficulties. He commented:

> Do you not know that *the business of life is a campaign*? One man must mount guard, another go out on reconnaissance, and another go out to fight . . . So also in this world; each man's life is a kind of campaign, and a long and complicated one at that. You have to maintain the character of a *soldier*.[6]

Epictetus uses the image of the soldier to communicate the tenacity one must have in facing the complexities that one experiences in life. Life, he argues, is like a long, hard, complicated campaign.

Likening life to the battle of a soldier is something we also find in the Old Testament writings. Throughout the Psalms the writers constantly use metaphoric images of battles, fights, and struggles.[7] Not only are individuals likened to fighting men, but the whole nation is also pictured as a fighting soldier. In Zechariah 9:13, for example, we read of Israel being like a "warrior's sword." Not only are individuals and their nation likened to a fighting soldier, but so also is God himself. We read in Exodus 15:3, "The Lord is a man of war; the Lord is his name."

In the ancient world the fighting warrior or soldier was seen as an important and necessary member of the community. The soldier, as we've observed, was also a positive metaphor of the type of person who would with tenacity, dedication, and commitment to a larger goal navigate their way through life's challenges. It is within this same mental framework that we see the Christian believer likened to a soldier in the New Testament.

THE CHRISTIAN AS A SOLDIER IN WAR IN THE NEW TESTAMENT

The New Testament Christian community existed in the context of a military world. Although there was an extended period of peace under the Romans, known as the *Pax Romana*, there was a strong military presence in most parts of the empire. Like the Old Testament writers and the Stoic philosophers, the New Testament writers present the soldier as a useful lens through which to view life.

---

6. Epictetus, *Discourses*, 3.31, 35 (Oldfather, trans.).

7. See, for example, (Pss 27:3; 35:1; 140:2).

Knowing Who You Are

Spiritual Soldiers

Thinking about the positive character traits of the soldier, Paul praised some of his fellow Christians by referring to them with that title. He writes:

> But I think it is necessary to send back to you Epaphroditus, my brother, co-worker and *fellow soldier*, who is also your messenger, whom you sent to take care of my needs. (Phil 2:25)

> . . . also to Apphia our sister and Archippus our *fellow soldier*—and to the church that meets in your home. (Phlm 2)

Epaphroditus and Archippus were, evidently, people who acted as devoted and faithful spiritual soldiers for Christ.

Just as the soldier fought hard in life so Paul exhorted his younger protégé Timothy to view his own life through the grid of soldier.

> Timothy, my son, I am giving you this command in keeping with the prophecies once made about you, so that by recalling them you may *fight the battle* well. (1 Tim 1:18)

Indeed, Paul used the language of the soldier about himself when, in his final letter, he states:

> Join with me in suffering, like *a good soldier* of Christ Jesus. No one serving as a soldier gets entangled in civilian affairs, but rather tries to please his commanding officer. (2 Tim 2:3)

Paul's "soldier" references would not have been lost on his first-century audience. All around them they would have seen soldiers who had devoted themselves to the emperor and his empire, soldiers who lived disciplined, devoted, and obedient lives. In light of this Paul contextualizes this image and uses it as a spiritual metaphor whereby Christians are to see themselves as spiritual soldiers of Christ. In the way that the Roman soldier was committed to his empire so also the Christians are to demonstrate equal devotion and loyalty, but to their king, Jesus. Concerning this Hobbs notes:

> Much of the language of advice to the Christian "soldier" takes on the tone of the soldier's oath, the *sacramentum*, which every Roman soldier had to take. Such an oath meant a radical change of life and a binding dedication to the service of the emperor.

The Christian as Soldier

Anything short of this was shameful, often punishable by death, and unworthy of an imperial soldier.[8]

A Spiritual War

Not only does the New Testament push us to see ourselves as spiritual soldiers committed in obedience to our commander Jesus, it also reveals the nature of our battle. The Christian life is not a battle between people but a spiritual one. Writing to the Ephesians Paul explains:

> ... our struggle is not against flesh and blood, but against the rulers, against the authorities, against the powers of this dark world and against the spiritual forces of evil in the heavenly realms. (Eph 6:12)

The battle we are in as followers of Christ is not a physical one. The opponent is not a visible person or country, but *spiritual forces*. There are at least three battles we wage at any one time in this spiritual conflict. Our war is against the world, the flesh, and the devil.

1. We War against the World

As soldiers of Christ one of the battles we wage is against the world. In the Scriptures, "the world" is representative of any framework that sets itself up in opposition to God. The "world" represents the mindset that minimizes the work of Christ and maximizes life apart from God. John warns about embracing the world when he writes:

> Do not love the world or anything in the world. If anyone loves the world, love for the Father is not in them. For everything in the world—the lust of the flesh, the lust of the eyes, and the pride of life—comes not from the Father but from the world. The world and its desires pass away, but whoever does the will of God lives forever. (1 John 2:15–17)

The world finds its origin back in the garden of Eden where Adam and Eve chose to disobey God and went after their own desires and lusts rather than obeying God. The problem of our forebears, however, is also the same

---

8. Hobbs, "War," 1366.

problem we face. Our natural disposition is to embrace life apart from God. All around us the world beckons us to follow its way of living for oneself. The world says live for money, self-gratification, and unashamed pleasure. The world says that God is *not* enough to bring contentment. Being products of this world our hearts urge us to be fiercely independent of God. To live in a way contrary to our natural disposition, therefore, requires from us the rigorous discipline of a good soldier.

When we reject the way of the world and fight against its worldview we will often feel ostracized. In our day when a person speaks up about God's view of sex, marriage, money, justice, abortion, or the environment, the world often reacts to the Christian with animosity. The world frequently mocks and shows disdain toward the servant of Christ. Jesus, however, anticipated this as he prayed for us in his high priestly prayer:

> I have given them your word and the world has hated them, for they are not of the world any more than I am of the world. My prayer is not that you take them out of the world but that you protect them from the evil one. (John 17:14–15)

If we are obedient servants of Christ we should expect opposition from the world. In fact Jesus said "in this world you *will* have trouble" (John 16:33). Antagonism toward the believer is a guaranteed facet of life. Like soldiers, however, we are to follow King Jesus as he calls us to live for his kingdom.

2. We War against the Flesh

The Christian soldier's war is not just an external one against the world that seeks to undermine Christ, but the battle is also an internal one that takes place in every believer's own heart. As mentioned previously, our natural tendency is to live independently of God. Our hearts are, as the hymn writer said, "prone to wander." Until the great resurrection day when Christ will fully change us we will struggle with mixed passion. In his letter to the Galatians the Apostle Paul articulates this conflict when he writes:

> So I say, walk by the Spirit, and you will not gratify the desires of the flesh. For the flesh desires what is contrary to the Spirit, and the Spirit what is contrary to the flesh. *They are in conflict with each other,* so that you are not to do whatever you want. But if you are led by the Spirit, you are not under the law. The acts of the

> flesh are obvious: sexual immorality, impurity and debauchery; idolatry and witchcraft; hatred, discord, jealousy, fits of rage, selfish ambition, dissensions, factions and envy; drunkenness, orgies, and the like. I warn you, as I did before, that those who live like this will not inherit the kingdom of God. But the fruit of the Spirit is love, joy, peace, forbearance, kindness, goodness, faithfulness, gentleness and self-control. Against such things there is no law. Those who belong to Christ Jesus have crucified the flesh with its passions and desires. (Gal 5:16–24)

The conflict within each one of us who follows Christ is the battle between our *fleshy desires* and the *Spirit of God*. God invites us to walk with him. When we live in step with him the result is the observable "fruit of the Spirit." If we don't walk in obedience, as a good soldier, the result will be indulgent fleshly living that will be equally as obvious. As Christ's soldiers the call of the Holy Spirit is to walk in step with God's desires as we listen to and obey commanding officer Jesus. As soldiers our allegiance is regularly tested, often by our own wayward nature, but we are to remain dedicated to our Master's cause and to soldier on.

3. We War against the Devil

The final war the believer is engaged in is the one against the "devil's schemes" (Eph 6:11). The "devil" is clearly our adversary just as he was Adam and Eve's in the garden; and just as with our forebears the father of lies seeks to derail our loyalty to King Jesus by seeking to coerce us into disobedience. In the garden the devil questioned Eve by raising doubts over the truthfulness of God's word. He said to Eve, "Did God *really* say . . . ?" (Gen 3:1). In a similar vein, Satan's ploy to unsettle our faith is by undermining the truth of God's wisdom in our day-to-day lives. He places seeds of doubt when he asks:

> Does God *really* say sex outside of marriage is wrong?
>
> Does God *really* say honesty is the best approach?
>
> Does God *really* say that lying is inappropriate for his children?
>
> Does God *really* say you should forgive someone who has wronged you?

The devil is spoken of in the New Testament as the one who tries to "trap" the child of God into rebellion against their Lord (1 Tim 3:6; 2 Tim 2:26). This one, whom Peter calls our "enemy" (1 Pet 5:8), seeks to devour us as a lion. Even our Lord Jesus Christ was not immune to the devil's testing as he too was tested by the evil one during his earthly ministry (Matt 4:1).

The good news of the gospel is that the devil's doom is assured (Rev 20:10). Our adversary, and the enemy of our soul, seeks to trap us but he will *never* defeat us. Until the final day of his judgment, however, he will seek to destroy our homes, marriages, and lives. As believers we must "resist the devil" (Jam 4:7) by trusting in Christ and standing firm against the schemes of the wicked one. As we stand our ground as obedient soldiers we should also pray to our Master that he would "deliver us from the evil one" (Matt 6:13).

WHAT CAN WE LEARN FROM THE SOLDIER?

A few years ago my wife Tamara and I had the privilege of being involved in some ministry in her native country of Ecuador. During our stay there we enjoyed spending time at a small Bible college right on the equator. This humble training institute was committed to equipping young indigenous men and women, from the Quechua, Shuar, and Huaorani tribes, for ministry in their jungle contexts. While spending time with the students I particularly fell in love with the Huaorani students. The Huaorani youth at this college were vibrant, easygoing, and well humored people. They were a far cry from their forebears who were formerly known by the unfortunate term of "auca," which means savage.

The Huaorani people, as is well documented, were responsible for the deaths of five young missionaries in the 1956. Nate Saint, Ed McCully, Peter Fleming, Roger Youderian, and Jim Elliot all died in their effort to reach the so-called "auca" with the gospel. As time progressed, however, through the faithful ministry of other believers the Huaorani were won to Christ and now Bible colleges, such as the one we ministered at, give evidence that the death of the five missionaries was not in vain. Indeed, as my wife and I spent time in the Ecuadorian jungle we could see firsthand what great things can happen as the result of great sacrifice.

A few years before I went to Ecuador I committed to reading through the diaries of one of the deceased missionaries, Jim Elliot. As I made my way through his reflections, published in the book *Through Gates of Splendor*, one thing stood out to me and that was the commitment of Jim and his fellow missionaries to the task of Christ. With an unwavering focus these families resolved to take the gospel to a place where Jesus had never been preached. The outcome of their devotion to the cause of Christ meant relocating from the comforts of everyday life in America to live in the harsh Ecuadorian jungle. The missionaries knew the difficult and costly task in front of them and in spite of this willingly shaped their lives around reaching the Huaorani people. These men and their wives wholeheartedly committed themselves to the mission of God and in their actions they concretely exemplified the Biblical image of the Christian as a "good soldier" of Christ.

Good soldiers, like the missionaries, are those who not only know their task but those who also obey the orders of their superior and execute the mission that is given. A good soldier has discipline, an awareness of the enemy, and a willingness to commit to the cause, regardless of the sacrifice. Given these things are true of the soldier it is easy to see how the New Testament reminds us to mirror such traits as we serve Christ. The follower of Jesus has been commissioned by the Master to go, serve, and reach people with the gospel. The soldier of Christ must sacrifice certain things to remain effective in battle. As well as this, the Christian soldier must remain vigilant if they are to complete their kingdom mission. If we are to reflect these soldier-like traits in our day-to-day experience there are three things we need to consistently remind ourselves.

1. Like Good Soldiers We Need To Develop a Wartime Mentality

War changes things. Whenever there is a conflict in the world inevitably those involved, even if indirectly, must change the way they live. Business temporarily ceases, schools close, holidays may be put on hold or even cancelled. When there is a war the circumstances of the individual within the warzone always change accordingly. As Christians we live in a warzone. There is a celestial spiritual battle that goes on which is not apparent to the eye, but is still powerfully real. Day by day we wage war against the world, the flesh, and the devil. Yet, in spite of this truth, many of us live not as though a battle is being waged, but as if we are on one long spring break. What we need is to be awakened from our spiritual slumber. We need to develop a wartime mentality.

Knowing Who You Are

The renowned mission strategist Ralph Winter challenges us to think through the wartime versus peacetime mentality when he writes:

> The Queen Mary, lying in repose in the harbor at Long Beach, California is a fascinating museum of the past. Used both as a luxury liner in peacetime and a troop transport during the Second World War, its present status as a museum the length of three football fields affords a stunning contrast between the lifestyles appropriate in peace and war. On one side of a partition you see the dining room reconstructed to depict the peacetime table setting that was appropriate to the wealthy patrons of high culture for whom a dazzling array of knives and forks and spoons held no mysteries. On the other side of the partition the evidences of wartime austerities are in sharp contrast. One metal tray with indentations replaces fifteen plates and saucers. Bunks eight tiers high explain how the peacetime capacity of 3000 passengers gave way to 15,000 troops on board in wartime. How repugnant to the peacetime masters this transformation must have been! To do it took a national emergency, of course. The survival of a nation depended upon it. The essence of the great commission today is that the survival of many millions of people depends on its fulfillment.[9]

How many of us as Christians live as though we are on a "peacetime" vacation? We live to own a home, or to raise a family, or to retire with sufficient money in the bank. The evil one deceives us into thinking that this life is it so we must grab as much satisfaction and pleasure as we can get. The net result is that we live to please ourselves and fail to see that we are in a spiritual conflict. We lay down our spiritual weapons and have no meaningful impact for the kingdom.

The soldier image should remind us of the basic yet often lost truth that we are in a spiritual war. Paul's exhortation to Timothy is something you and I need to constantly put before ourselves.

> Join with me in suffering, like *a good soldier* of Christ Jesus. No one serving as a soldier gets entangled in civilian affairs, but rather tries to please his commanding officer. (2 Tim 2:3)

If you are anything like me you are tempted to get "entangled in civilian affairs." We stumble and get trapped by the things that often have very little bearing on eternity. We forget our "commanding officer" and make our

---

9. Quoted in Piper, *Don't Waste Your Life*, 112–114.

own decisions as if we were in charge. From our independence we must repent and re-engage with the battle.

Living with a wartime mentality does not necessarily mean that we will drop everything and leave for a remote mission field, though for some that is appropriate. Living with a wartime mentality means living with Christ's kingdom agenda firmly in mind. This might mean reshaping the ways I think about how I use my career, free time, and even money. As a spiritual soldier I might view time spent with young Christians as *strategic* training rather than viewing it as an *inconvenience*. Rather than spending "me time" on my own leisure and hobbies, I might choose to systematically visit and encourage older folks from my church. Rather than using money for my own benefit, I might sacrificially give to support those in need. Rather than using my "golden years" for retirement I might offer my time to volunteer in a soup kitchen. If we think Christ's kingdom and glory are ultimate we must surely respond by reprioritizing our goals around his command and mission, not around our own. We must remember we are in a battle.

2. Like Good Soldiers We Must Obey Our Commander

In the ancient world, as with now, the military worked on a ranking system. Soldiers in biblical times were not free agents who did as they pleased, but were those under authority. Nowadays it is the same. If a training officer barks out orders to run three miles, or to give fifty pushups, the soldier is not in the position to object or to challenge the officer's wisdom. Rather, the good and wise soldier does as they are told first time.

As mentioned previously our natural tendency, which we must war against, is the fleshy notion that we are ultimate authorities over our lives. In the great commission Jesus provides the mandate to "go and make disciples of all nations" (Matt 28:19). Jesus does not say:

> "*if you have a bit of spare time* then go and make disciples . . ."
>
> "*if you have extra financial resources* then go and make disciples . . ."
>
> "*if you've paid off your house* then go and make disciples . . ."
>
> "*if you've got your children through school* then go and make disciples . . ."

Our commander and chief calls us to follow him in his great mission of making God's glory known to all humanity. Given Jesus' authority, anything less than obedience misunderstands or willingly ignores his necessary lordship over our lives. Jesus does not give us all the same gifts, or abilities, or tasks in his mission, but he does desire that whatever our occupation, whether as a school teacher, electrician, or nurse, and whatever our marital status, whether single, married, or divorced, and whatever our age, be it as a teenager, middle aged, or twilight years, that we recognize that his agenda still needs to be our top priority. Jesus is not a harsh commander who will force our hand, but he is a loving leader who calls us to his task. The soldier image reminds us that we must keep in the battle as we follow Jesus' directions.

3. Like Good Soldiers We Must Arm Ourselves for Battle

Remembering that we are soldiers is important; knowing our commander and his mission is crucial; but if we are to be effective soldiers for Christ it is imperative that we prepare ourselves for battle. Just as it would be foolish to turn up to a gunfight with a knife, so it would be highly unwise to be in a spiritual battle without the right protection. Fortunately for us, however, the Apostle Paul addressed the Ephesian church on how to approach this exact task. He wrote:

> Finally, be strong in the Lord and in his mighty power. Put on the full armor of God, so that you can take your stand against the devil's schemes. For our struggle is not against flesh and blood, but against the rulers, against the authorities, against the powers of this dark world and against the spiritual forces of evil in the heavenly realms. Therefore put on the full armor of God, so that when the day of evil comes, you may be able to stand your ground, and after you have done everything, to stand. Stand firm then, with the belt of truth buckled around your waist, with the breastplate of righteousness in place, and with your feet fitted with the readiness that comes from the gospel of peace. In addition to all this, take up the shield of faith, with which you can extinguish all the flaming arrows of the evil one. Take the helmet of salvation and the sword of the Spirit, which is the word of God. (Eph 6:10–17)

In this passage Paul provides a helpful and immensely practical approach to spiritual warfare. Rather than talking in mystical vagaries, as many contemporary people do, Paul, having identified that our struggle is

The Christian as Soldier

against "spiritual forces of evil in the heavenly realms," provides a wonderful picture that helps us see how we can "stand" for King Jesus.

The first thing I notice in this passage is that we need to find our strength "in the Lord and his mighty power" (6:10). The power of the Christian is not found in "rebuking the devil," as not even Michael the archangel did this (Jude 9), but in the strength of trusting our all-powerful God. Often when people talk of spiritual encounters and battles they think power lies in mantras, special prayers, and the like, but this passage reminds me that spiritual power is founding in resting in Christ. When I am warring against the world, my flesh, or the devil, rather than fighting a losing battle in my own strength I must simply cast myself at Jesus' feet and depend upon him to strengthen me.

Regularly I meet fellow Christian soldiers who are discouraged in their spiritual battle. Whether it is the young man wrestling with pornography, the middle-aged woman who can't forgive herself for a sin of the past, or the older person living with deep regrets, all of us grow weary in our battle. What I continue to discover, however, is that regardless of age or type of struggle, if we simply try new techniques to modify our behavior or thoughts nothing will change. Spiritual victory has been achieved in the finished work of Jesus. It is *not* achieved through well meaning human efforts. When you and I remind ourselves that we are "in the Lord" and when we identity with him, it doesn't matter what we've done, we can't be shaken. Our battle is real, but Christ is the one who provides victory, not our own feeble efforts of resistance. As we walk in step with our Lord he provides us with the power to overcome the enemies of the world, the flesh, and the devil.

But how do we "stand in the Lord"? Paul gives the answer by way of illustration as he refers to a soldier's fighting armor. We are to put on the "full armor of God" (6:11). Now I'm not sure the last time you put on armor, but it is quite involved. Recently my family and I were holidaying in bonnie Scotland. While there we visited the impressive Edinburgh Castle. While walking around the castle grounds we stopped to hear an explanation of the ancient fighting methods of the Scottish soldiers. When they asked for a volunteer to put on the fighting gear for the demonstration my hand went straight up, much to the delight of my children. Before I knew it I was facing one hundred and fifty people wearing a heavy metal helmet and an impregnable chain suit, and was brandishing a large metal sword. I was ready to be the next William Wallace! The thing that surprised me was the amount of time it took to get prepared and the significance of every part of the armor.

Dressing oneself in armor takes effort and intention. You don't simply slip on a heavy metal vest, it requires work. Similarly, our preparation for battle requires intentionality. You must have "the belt of truth buckled around your waist" (6:14). The soldier wore a belt for many reasons. The belt kept the garments secure, it acted as a place to hold the sword, and if strong enough could protect the thighs. Although it was often unsighted, the belt held things together. As believers the thing that is to bring all of our life together is the "belt of truth." At the very core of everything we do must be the knowledge of who Christ is, and who we are in relation to him. When we undergird our lives with biblical truth it provides stability in the battles of life. As one writer said, "As believers internalize God's truth they live and move in it."[10]

The spiritual soldier must also have "the breastplate of righteousness in place" (6:14). The breastplate was a metal plate worn over the soldier's garments that was designed to protect the torso and in particular the heart from the strike of a sword. The breastplate was not an offensive weapon, but a defensive protective device. For the believer the protective device that will keep our enemy at bay is righteousness. When we actively live out the righteous life God has given us we protect ourselves spiritually. When we "submit to God" we are able to "resist the devil" (Jam 4:7). Spiritual resistance against our enemy is best accomplished by walking in righteousness. This lifestyle should hang over us like a breastplate.

We are also to add to this armor the right spiritual footwear. Our feet are to be "fitted with the readiness that comes from the gospel of peace" (6:15). Shoes were an important part of the soldier's defense. One writer explains:

> The Roman legionaries wore heavy sandals (*caliga,* a low half-boot) with soles made of several layers of leather averaging 3 centimeters (3/4 inch) thick, studded with hollow-headed hobnails. They were tied by leather thongs half-way up the shin and were stuffed with wool or fur for the cold weather . . . These were not running sandals but ones able to dig in with their hollow-headed hobnails and stand against the enemy.[11]

---

10. Hoehner, *Ephesians*, 840.
11. Ibid., 842.

The Christian as Soldier

The boots, like the belt and breastplate, are not instruments of attack, but of defense. In order to protect oneself one must have the surefootedness of the gospel. The image is not so much one of taking the gospel out as much as it is having a clear and firm reliance on the message of the gospel. When you and I are discouraged and thinking of quitting, coming back to the truth of the gospel will help us to remain firm. Even in the midst of spiritual war the gospel still brings us "peace."

We are to add to this spiritual armor the "shield of faith" (6:16) and "the helmet of salvation" (6:17). The "shield of faith" indicates a resolute trust. For the believer an unwavering belief in the finished work of the cross provides spiritual protection from the "fiery darts" of the evil one. Similarly, the helmet of salvation gives the believer confidence that no foe or circumstance can deliver a deathblow to them.

The final piece of the soldier's armor presented in this image is the "sword of the Spirit, which is the word of God" (6:17). Out of all the instruments listed this is the only offensive one. Even though the soldier's sword was used to strike the opponent, the context is not one of aggression but defense. The believer is not out to destroy with the sword, but to defend with the sword. The sword believers have is the "word of God." Just as Jesus defended himself from temptation through the recitation of Scripture, so likewise the effective soldier of Christ knows and applies the Scriptures to their own soul when facing the enemy.

The emphasis in Paul's illustration of the soldier's armor is clear. The believer and their war are not about proactively seeking spiritual battles, rather this is about *standing firm*. The world, the flesh, and the devil actively seek to bring us harm and to destroy us. How are we to respond in spiritual warfare? We are to "stand firm" by trusting in the Lord's power as we actively remind ourselves of the gospel. Spiritual warfare is not about mystical mantras or special prayers, it is about being a soldier willing to live a godly and consistent life for the Master, a life that is perpetually refined by the gospel. As we stand firm in active godliness the gospel progresses.

In perhaps his most famous hymn the reformer Martin Luther encapsulated the nature of our spiritual battle. Though based on Psalm 46, the cosmic type of our combat, our role as soldiers, and the victory obtained by Christ echo through the song. As soldiers of Christ we would do well to remind ourselves of these truths as we "stand firm" for the gospel delivered to us.

A mighty fortress is our God, a bulwark never failing;

Knowing Who You Are

our helper he amid the flood of mortal ills prevailing.
For still our ancient foe doth seek to work us woe;
his craft and power are great, and armed with cruel hate,
on earth is not his equal.

Did we in our own strength confide, our striving would be losing,
were not the right man on our side, the man of God's own choosing.
Dost ask who that may be? Christ Jesus, it is he;
Lord Sabaoth, his name, from age to age the same, and he must win the battle.

And though this world, with devils filled, should threaten to undo us,
we will not fear, for God hath willed his truth to triumph through us.
The Prince of Darkness grim, we tremble not for him;
his rage we can endure, for lo, his doom is sure;
one little word shall fell him.

That word above all earthly powers, no thanks to them, abideth;
the Spirit and the gifts are ours, thru him who with us sideth.
Let goods and kindred go, this mortal life also;
the body they may kill; God's truth abideth still;
his kingdom is forever.

REFLECTIONS

1. The ancient soldier's life was characterized by tenacity, discipline, and obedience to the commander. In following Master Jesus as a good soldier which do you need to work on the most?
2. Our spiritual battle is one against the world, the flesh, and the devil. Which of these opponents do you wrestle with most? What is a good battle plan for you to stand firm in your struggle?
3. Finish this statement. "Lord help me as a good soldier to . . . "
4. Often it is easy to forget we are in a spiritual warzone. How does your mentality need to change as the result of knowing you are in a battle *not* on a spiritual holiday?

PRAYER

> Sovereign God,
> Thank you that you have counted us worthy to be soldiers in your service. We are humbled that you would include us to accomplish your glorious plans for the world. Enable us to remain focused on our tasks. Help us, as good soldiers, to be disciplined, obedient, and tenaciously committed to executing your mission to reach the world. Grant us boldness, courage, and strength as we serve. Forgive us for becoming ensnared by the world, the flesh, and the devil. Grant us focus as we discern what you are doing in the world. As we commit to your campaign may we remain true to your cause. No matter the cost. We ask this for Jesus' sake.
> Amen.

8

The Christian as Laborer

> "We often miss opportunity because it's dressed in overalls and looks like work."
> —THOMAS EDISON

> "Therefore, my dear brothers and sisters, stand firm. Let nothing move you. Always give yourselves fully to the work of the Lord, because you know that your labor in the Lord is not in vain."
> —1 CORINTHIANS 15:58

> "And whatever you do, whether in word or deed, do it all in the name of the Lord Jesus, giving thanks to God the Father through him."
> —COLOSSIANS 3:17

I LOVE LEGO. ALWAYS have. Always will. Ever since I can remember I have always enjoyed playing with the little colored blocks. I am, however, not the only one. Since its inception in Denmark in 1949 the exponential popularity of these small interlocking bricks has been staggering, to the point that there now exist over 560 billion pieces of Lego worldwide! Based on the ideals of imagination, creativity, fun, learning, caring, and quality, Lego continues to entertain men, women, and children of all ages in every culture. People all over the globe love Lego.

The Christian as Laborer

In our home at Christmas time or for birthdays Lego is usually somewhere near the top of the gift list. The nice part about that is that I am often called on to help assemble the pieces. A year or two ago my son asked me to help put together a large Lego Star Wars ship of over a thousand pieces! I set to the task. I painstakingly followed the instructions of the book page by page under the careful observation of my young protégé. I put it together piece by piece and after three long hours sat back with my son Adam and marveled at the completed Millennium Falcon. It was very satisfying.

One of the reasons we find Lego enjoyable is because it enables us to work on a project that we can see come to completion. Being able to accomplish a task that requires patience, attention to detail, skill, and mental acumen is rewarding. Working with our hands and minds produces within us a positive sense of pride and purpose. I would submit to you that the reason we feel this way has more than just Lego to it. I would argue that you and I find a sense of purpose and reward in working because that is what you and I have been created to do.

For many people work is seen as a necessary evil. Work, it is felt, is simply something people must do to provide for themselves and others. The Bible, however, portrays work as a significant and holy thing. In the Genesis account of creation, for example, Adam is given work to do in naming the animals *before* he has fallen into sin. God gave Adam work to do and it was good and purposeful. Work, as originally intended, was not to be a burden but a delight.

Over time people, including Christians, have often divided the world into two false categories of the "sacred" and the "secular." "Sacred" activities have often been limited to things like church, praying, and communal worship. Other areas of life like studying, shopping, farming, and working have often been viewed as "secular," non-spiritual things. The Bible, however, presents all of life as "sacred." To God our work on a Monday is just as significant as our church life on a Sunday. For God "work" is an important part of our design and an extension of our worship.

When we understand that all of life is sacred and that every task, be it small or large, is part of life under God we enter the liberating truth that frees us to delight in all things. Paul writing to the Colossians put it this way:

> And whatever you do, whether in word or deed, do it all in the name of the Lord Jesus, giving thanks to God the Father through him. (3:17)

Whether teaching second grade children, assembling cars, pastoring a church, or crunching numbers in a tax office, our work is worship. Redeeming the value of work is important to understanding ourselves. No matter how God has wired us, he has given us certain talents and abilities with the purpose that we might joyfully serve him. Work in the creation order of God is a valuable and intentional thing.

One of the reasons it is important to think about the worker and their work is because the Bible uses metaphoric language of work in regard to Christian discipleship. The Scripture's positive presentation of the worker and their work provides helpful metaphors from which we can better understand both our Christian identity and our God-given purpose in life. In light of the broad use of the worker and work imagery in the New Testament, it would be helpful to overview how the Christian is like a "worker" before looking at two biblical examples of working that we can learn from.

THE CHRISTIAN AS LABORER

My first ever job was working in a movie theater. I would like to say it was an important position selling tickets, or providing popcorn to the patrons, but it wasn't. My job was to scour the floors after the movie with a flashlight and garbage bag to pick up the rubbish. It wasn't the most creative job in the world but it paid a whopping five dollars per hour, which made me very happy. I have worked in a variety of occupations during my life, from movie theater garbage collector to graphic designer, from computer support to serving as a church pastor. Over the course of time I've found work to be both engaging at times while much more mundane at others. In all of my working life, however, I've noticed that three things stand out about work. Work requires effort, consistency, and perseverance.

Work Requires Effort

In the New Testament the Christian life and ministry are pictured as "work" and each of the traits that are true of an effective employee in today's workplace are traits that are appropriate in our working for the Lord. Like our day-to-day professions, to be effective workers requires that we first of all apply effort. Consider, for example, the following verses.

The Christian as Laborer

> Therefore, my dear brothers and sisters, stand firm. Let nothing move you. Always give yourselves fully to the work of the Lord, because you know that your *labor* in the Lord is not in vain. (1 Cor 15:58)

> Now we ask you, brothers and sisters, to acknowledge those who *work hard* among you, who care for you in the Lord and who admonish you. Hold them in the highest regard in love because of their *work*. Live in peace with each other. (1 Thess 5:12–13)

Just as nurses spend late nights caring for the ill, and tax agents crunch numbers on the brink of the new financial year, so effective Christians toil, strive, "labor," and "work hard" for their Master. The Christian life, like an occupation, doesn't flourish unless hours of discipline, intentionality, and effort are poured in. Christians, contrary to the opinion of some, are not to be lazy, pie-in-the-sky type people, but diligent, focused, and hardworking people. People like these were esteemed in the early church. We read:

> Greet Mary, *who worked very hard* for you. (Rom 16:6)

> Greet Tryphena and Tryphosa, those women *who work hard* in the Lord. Greet my dear friend Persis, another woman *who has worked very hard* in the Lord. (Rom 16:12)

> I vouch for him [Epaphras] that *he is working hard* for you and for those at Laodicea and Hierapolis. (Col 4:13)

As Christians we are to serve the Lord, in whatever role we have, with tenacity and effort. The reason we are to do this is because we have been created for this purpose.

> For we are God's handiwork, created in Christ Jesus *to do good works*, which God prepared in advance for us to do. (Eph 2:10)

While we are appropriately accountable to our human employers, we are to remember that ultimately we are employees of the living God. As Paul reminds us:

> Whatever you do, work at it with all your heart, as *working for the Lord*, not for human masters. (Col 3:23)

Knowing Who You Are

Work Requires Consistency

The Christian life not only requires hard work, it also requires an element of consistency. Reliability and loyalty are important facets of all businesses that succeed. Often companies that flourish are not those staffed by the greatest or most gifted people. They are the ones who have a reliable staff who are committed long term to seeing the company's goals reached. In a similar manner effective employees of the Lord are not always the flashy or the most gifted members of the community, but simply those who plug away faithfully at their God-given tasks. Writing to the Corinthian church Paul reminds them of their calling:

> Brothers and sisters, think of what you were when you were called. Not many of you were wise by human standards; not many were influential; not many were of noble birth. But God chose the foolish things of the world to shame the wise; God chose the weak things of the world to shame the strong. (1 Cor 1:26–27)

God's employment roster is not made up of an A-list of celebrities and powerful people. God uses ordinary, everyday-type people for his work. The key to his work, however, is not the gifting of his worker as much as it is the worker's commitment to the Master's plan. There is great power when the people of God simply and quietly live out what they believe. Not only does God notice when we do this, but also the world around us takes note.

> In the same way, let your light shine before others, that they may *see your good deeds* and glorify your Father in heaven. (Matt 5:16)

> Live such good lives among the pagans that, though they accuse you of doing wrong, they may *see your good deeds* and glorify God on the day he visits us. (1 Pet 2:12)

As a young Christian I would sometimes hear a well meaning evangelist or pastor share a testimony from the front of the church as to how they caught the bus earlier in the week and three stops after getting on the bus they had led four people to the Lord including the bus driver! I would sit there, drop my head, and think, "I can't do that." I mistakenly believed that God's work was only that which involved leading people to pray the "sinner's prayer." I have since discovered that God's work is so much more than that. God's work is best proclaimed from a character which consistently mirrors a genuine righteousness produced by the Holy Spirit. Obviously we look for opportunities to verbally share God's goodness, but we must never underestimate the power that is found in simply working hard with our hearts, hands, and minds to show that in every area of life Jesus Christ is Lord.

Work Requires Perseverance

As employees of God our service for him requires intentionality and effort. It also, we have discovered, requires consistency of character. Lastly, being God's workers also requires perseverance. When you work for God there are times when service feels mundane, boring, and perhaps even fruitless. At such times we often feel like taking the easier route, not applying ourselves, viewing our work as a "secular" necessity rather than a "sacred" opportunity. Just as an employer values a long-term employee, so also God does not forget those who remain committed to his service.

The church of Ephesus was one that labored long and hard for the gospel. Jesus said to the church:

> I know your works, your toil and your *patient endurance*, and how you cannot bear with those who are evil, but have tested those who call themselves apostles and are not, and found them to be false. I know you are *enduring patiently* and *bearing up* for my name's sake, and you have not grown weary. (Rev 2:2–3)

The Ephesians underwent all sorts of trials and there were no doubt moments of discouragement, yet they were praised for "patient endurance" and not growing "weary." The church labored for the Master in light of the long term. I imagine they did not always *feel* like their work was fruitful, but in faith they kept plowing along. Often ministry is like that. Faithfully living out our faith in our occupations whether as a dentist, an educator, an electrician, or a pastor does not always feel fruitful or significant, yet if we work as unto the Lord the Bible says our "labor is not in vain" (1 Cor 15:58). For the Ephesians, persevering in their service for the Lord would culminate in reward, not necessarily in this life, but certainly in the life to come. Jesus promised:

> To the one who conquers I will grant to eat of the tree of life, which is in the paradise of God. (Rev 2:7)

The Scriptures remind us that we have been "created in Christ Jesus to do *good works*" (Eph 2:9). The mundaneness of doing these "good works" for the Lord in every sphere of life may not feel rewarding, but in faith we must obediently persevere. As long-term employees of the Lord we must be committed to his larger vision for his creation, not just our short-term plans.

In the New Testament many different occupations are referred to. Of these occupations there are two that I would like to focus on as they reflect the ideals God is seeking to cultivate in the Christian as a laborer. The builder and the fisherman are images used of those following Christ that are helpful in thinking about our Christian identity.

THE CHRISTIAN LABORS LIKE A BUILDER

Recently my family and I had the chance to travel through Israel. My wife and I have been to Israel many times and always enjoy visiting the Holy Land. As this was the first time our children had been we were keen to gauge their impressions. During the course of our visit many things stood out. They delighted in the narrow streets of the Old City of Jerusalem, loved floating in the Dead Sea, and appreciated the beauty of the fertile Galilee region. Of the many things they enjoyed, however, high on their list of amazement were the large and very impressive buildings constructed by Herod the Great. The fortress of Masada, the large walls of Jerusalem, and the ancient city of Caesarea on the coast were constantly met with "whoa!" King Herod was a terrible man, but was clearly known as "great" because of these building endeavors.

As we stood at the ruins of Caesarea on the Mediterranean coast I contemplated the significant role of the builder in ancient times. Jesus, himself a builder (Mark 6:3), was certainly familiar with the intricacies of constructing an edifice and often likened the life of a Christian to this occupation. Jesus taught:

> Therefore everyone who hears these words of mine and puts them into practice is like a wise man who *built* his house on the rock. The rain came down, the streams rose, and the winds blew and beat against that house; yet it did not fall, because it had its foundation on the rock. But everyone who hears these words of mine and does not put them into practice is like a foolish man who *built* his house on sand. The rain came down, the streams rose, and the winds blew and beat against that house, and it fell with a great crash. (Matt 7:24–27)

In context, Jesus' illustration of the builder is at the end of his famous "Sermon on the Mount." Wanting to make clear the importance of responding in obedience to his teaching, he pointed out the difference between wisdom and folly. The wise person in the story is not one who simply knows how to construct a house, but one who builds the structure on the *right* foundation. Jesus without hesitation claims that his teaching is that right foundation. He is saying, in essence, if you want to build your life in the right way, the godly way, then base it on his teachings.

As Christians it is imperative that we, like the wise builder, have Jesus' teaching at the very foundation of our lives. All areas of life, career, money, and relationships, should be shaped around his wisdom. If we fail to listen to Jesus and build our lives around our own knowledge then we are, as it were, constructing a building that is doomed to fail when times of testing come.

In our lives we are never quite sure when the storms will come. For me the storm of cancer came seven years ago. I never expected this to happen to me, but the storm came, and I mean it *really* came. During this difficult time of testing one of the things that kept me going was the fact that over the course of my life I, through the grace of God, had laid a solid platform of truth based on the teachings of the Bible. Issues such as God's sovereignty, his faithful love, and joy in the midst of suffering, came to the fore even though the rains came. My life was not without trouble, yet through the constant reminders of Scripture I was able to endure the difficulties. A good foundation will do that. For me, the theological training that had impacted my head now held my heart in good stead as I weathered the storm.

Storms will come and go in our lives. When a storm comes, however, it will test your foundations. While there are many useful resources out there, many good friends, much wisdom we can glean from others, there is nothing that can help us like knowing the will of God as revealed in Scripture. When you receive that phone call, or that diagnosis, or learn of tragedy, what will be your platform and foundation? If it is not Christ, you will be in danger of complete collapse.

The wise builder reminds us of the importance of a good foundation. As I looked out on where Herod had once built a port from Caesarea I could see that, though there were still remnants of the port underwater, the majority of his buildings had been washed away. There is folly in building on the sand; edifices that last are those with foundations built on the rock.

Knowing Who You Are

A second thing that we can learn from the builder is the importance of careful planning. In teaching about discipleship Jesus explained:

> Suppose one of you wants to build a tower. Won't you first sit down and estimate the cost to see if you have enough money to complete it? For if you lay the foundation and are not able to finish it, everyone who sees it will ridicule you, saying, "This person began to build and wasn't able to finish."(Luke 14:28–30)

Being a disciple of Jesus, like being a builder, requires careful consideration and should not be entered into lightly. In Jesus' day there were many who wanted to follow him. Of the large crowds, however, many were following him out of selfish motive. Some perhaps followed him hoping for a free meal, others perhaps in order to have an ailment healed. Jesus, however, taught that being a disciple was not a free-and-easy life but one of hard work. Being his disciple was not for the faint of heart, it was a difficult path to follow.

The image of the builder was to challenge those who were thinking of following him. Just as a builder should "first sit down and estimate the cost," so those who would follow Jesus must first stop and think through the commitment it requires. The builder who begins a tower and then runs out of material is embarrassed because the task is left undone and the structure incomplete. In a similar manner, the one wanting to follow Christ must carefully think through the decision. Jesus is not looking merely for converts, but long-term followers.

A few years ago I was speaking at a youth camp where there was plenty of free time to enjoy the activities of the campsite. For my afternoon retreat I decided to do canoeing. I made my way down to the jetty and, after strapping on the life jacket, I tried to get in the canoe. I say "tried" because that is exactly what I did. Canoeing is a fun activity but I am convinced the hardest part of the sport is actually getting in the canoe. As I put one foot in the canoe it began to shift away from the jetty. While the jetty was firm, the canoe seemed to have a mind of its own. At one point I had a foot on the jetty, the other on the canoe, and I could see my reflection in the water! I quickly realized that I couldn't waver between the two. I was either *all* on the jetty, or I needed to be *all* in the canoe. Anything less would end in disaster. For the Christian, the same commitment is required. We can build our lives on Christ, or build our lives on our own wisdom, but *not* on both.

Jesus' image of the carefully planning builder reminds us of the importance of following him with utter commitment. Being a disciple impacts

The Christian as Laborer

how you spend your money, whom you marry, and how you relate to your employer. Jesus is not just to be the Lord on Sunday, but also on Monday through Saturday. The builder reminds us of the importance of not rushing into commitment, but weighing up the cost carefully. Jesus' call is to carefully and definitively commit to his agenda. Anything less will not do.

THE CHRISTIAN LABORS LIKE A FISHERMAN

The Sea of Galilee is perhaps my most favorite place in Israel. In contrast to the dusty, loud, hustle-and-bustle feel of Jerusalem, the Sea of Galilee and its surrounding hills are green, lush, and marvelously serene. The beauty of the lake is echoed in Josephus' description of it. Writing during the New Testament era he commented,

> . . . its waters are sweet, and very agreeable for drinking, for they are finer than the thick waters of other fens; the lake is also pure, and on every side ends directly at the shores, and at the sand; it is also of a temperate nature when you draw it up, and of a more gentle nature than river or fountain water, and yet always cooler than one could expect in so diffuse a place as this is.[1]

Elsewhere Josephus concluded that the regions of Galilee with its bountiful water and fertile soil were the "the ambition of nature."[2] Clearly not much has changed from Josephus' day until now. Galilee still continues to be a wonderfully productive and tranquil part of Israel.

It is at this large mass of water and the towns lying around it that much of the ministry of Jesus took place. Jesus taught from a hill on the shore of Galilee (Matt 5:1), as well as from a boat on the Sea itself (Matt 13:2). He healed throughout the Galilean villages (Matt 4:23), fed thousands (Matt 14:21), calmed the raging Sea (Mark 4:39), and even lived there for a time (Matt 4:13). After his resurrection Jesus returned to the Galilee to entrust his mission to the disciples (Mark 16:7). Clearly the Sea of Galilee and its related towns were part of Jesus' everyday life.

Given Jesus' familiarity with the lifestyle of those living around the Sea of Galilee it should come as no surprise that he would employ many images from day-to-day life to communicate his message. One such occasion is recorded by Matthew:

1. Josephus, *The Jewish War*, 3.506–507 (Thackeray, trans.).
2. Ibid., 3.518.

Knowing Who You Are

> As Jesus was walking beside the Sea of Galilee he saw two brothers, Simon called Peter and his brother Andrew. They were casting a net into the lake, for they were fishermen. "Come, follow me," Jesus said, "and I will send you out to fish for people." At once they left their nets and followed him. (Matt 4:18–20)

Out of all the occupations Jesus could have called people from, fishing is surely one the modern reader would *not* expect. A lawyer would be a good choice, or maybe a young rabbi-in-training, an esteemed judge, or civic leader, but no, Jesus chose the everyday fisherman to be his disciple.

Galilee was replete with both fish and fishermen in the first century. Josephus recorded of the lake that there were "several kinds of fish in it, different both to the taste and the sight from those elsewhere."[3] He also noted as many as two hundred and thirty boats could be found out on the lake at any one time.[4] Fishing was big business. So though it takes the modern reader by surprise that Jesus would choose fishermen to be his disciples, it would not have been completely out of the ordinary for those in the first century. What is unusual about Jesus' call of the fisherman, however, is his now famous statement that he would make his disciple go out to "fish for people" (Matt 4:19).

Jesus' call to make his disciples "fish for people" is something that can easily be misunderstood. More than one well intentioned preacher has taken this to mean that the Christian's job is to go out with the attractive bait of the gospel, lure the fish, then reel them into praying the sinner's prayer. While there is nothing wrong with that desire, it is not really an adequate understanding of the image because it has begun with a misunderstanding of how the ancient fisherman actually went about catching fish.

In Bible times fishing was not a sport one would do for recreation, but an occupation that required hard work and patience. Fishermen then, unlike now, didn't use tackle, bait, and lightweight rods, their technique was far simpler. One scholar explains the process:

> The "cast net" was used by a single fisherman. It was circular, about 20–25 feet in diameter, with lead sinkers attached to the outer edge. Gathering the net on his arm, the fisherman would throw it out onto the water, either while standing in a boat or in shallow water. The net was pulled down by the sinkers on the outer ring

---

3. Ibid., 3.508.
4. Ibid., 2.65.

(like a parachute), sinking to the bottom with fish trapped inside. This is tedious work.[5]

As we can see, the fisherman would simply cast his net in a body of water and drag it back on board hoping that the net would have secured a few fish in the fine nets. Fishing was monotonous work with mixed results. It is this style of fishing that Jesus had in mind when he called his followers to "fish for people."

So what does it look like for the modern believer to "fish for people"? Fishing for people means spreading the gospel net as far and wide as we can. We never know who will respond to God's message but we must do our best to give people a chance. Fishing for people, like fishing for fish, requires both effort and patience. We know of several accounts in the Gospels where the seasoned fishermen let down their nets, only to catch nothing (cf. John 21:3). In a similar manner when we cast the net of the gospel there will be times when it seems like the pond is dry and there are no fish. With Jesus' help, however, there will be other times when God may bring in many fish, just as he literally did for the disciples (cf. John 21:6).

One of the things about fishing with the net in biblical times was that there were many different places to throw the net. Not everybody cast their net in the same part of the lake. In the same way as believers, we too are given different spheres of life in which to fish. As a fisher of people God has placed you in unique relationship with your own family, and your own realm of influence. The most effective spiritual fishing among business professionals is probably not the pastor of a church but the committed businessman or woman who loves the Lord and serves faithfully in that context. It is the godly school principal reaching other teachers in their context. It is the young mother raising infants fishing among other young mothers in her network. I fish for people in my context where you fish for others in yours. Our goal is the same, bringing people into God's kingdom, but our opportunities are diverse. Being like a fisherman involves regularly casting the net and doing it in whatever places we find ourselves. God is ultimately the one who sorts the fish, but our service is the means by which he catches them.

---

5. Wilkins, *Matthew*, 176–77.

Knowing Who You Are

WHAT CAN WE LEARN FROM THE BUILDER AND FISHERMAN?

During my early twenties I lived in the great city of Chicago. I loved the pace of the city, its music, and its basketball team the Chicago Bulls. One of the most impressive things about the city of Chicago, however, is its skyline. With both its diverse architecture and massive array of large buildings, the city provides a beautiful backdrop to Lake Michigan. Chicago and its buildings are very impressive.

During my time living in Chicago I discovered that underneath every large and tall building was a well constructed foundation. For every building that soared into the heavens, there was a foundation cut deep into the rock below the ground. Before a structure went up, an underlying base, sometimes many stories deep, would have to be prepared. All great buildings have strong foundations.

Like the Builder Know Your Foundation

The follower of Jesus, like a building, needs a firm foundation if they are to endure the tests of time. Just as the foundation of a building built upon rock provides a fixed base that can handle storms, earthquakes, and the elements, so also the life connected to Jesus that is built upon his teaching provides a security that can't be shaken. Paul exhorts us to build on this foundation when he writes:

> So then, just as you received Christ Jesus as Lord, continue to live your lives in him, rooted and *built up* in him, strengthened in the faith as you were taught, and overflowing with thankfulness. (Col 2:6–7)

Like the wise man of Jesus' story in Matthew 7 who built his house upon the rock so too we are to build our lives on the immovable rock of Jesus' teaching, not upon the shifting sands of earthly wisdom. As well as this, we are not only to build good foundations in our own lives, but we are also to help others remain firm by building into their lives as well.

> For we are co-workers in God's service; you are God's field, God's building. By the grace God has given me, I laid a foundation as a *wise builder*, and someone else is *building* on it. But each one should *build* with care. (1 Cor 3:9–11)

> Do not let any unwholesome talk come out of your mouths, but only what is helpful for *building others up* according to their needs, that it may benefit those who listen. (Eph 4:29)
>
> Therefore encourage one another and *build each other up*, just as in fact you are doing. (1 Thes 5:11)

As we reflect on the builder we must ask ourselves the questions, whose life are we building into? Who are we helping to prepare and strengthen to face the storm? In your own life how, like the builder, are you wisely and carefully shaping your life around God's master building plan or are you building your own little kingdom? The ancient builder calls us to work hard knowing that our "labor is not in vain in the Lord" (1 Cor 15:58).

Like the Fisherman Cast Your Nets Widely

It is surprising to many, but the earliest symbol connected with Christians was not the cross, but the fish. The "Christian fish," nowadays found on many car bumper stickers, was the most common symbol for the early Christians for a few reasons. First, the "fish and the loaves" represented Jesus' feeding of the multitudes. The popularity of this miracle resulted in many using this symbol to represent the power of Jesus. Second, the Greek word for fish (*Ichthus*) was, for some Christians, a useful acronym that stood for Jesus (*Iesus*), Christ (*Christos*), God (*Theos*), Son (*Huios*), Savior (*Soter*). Third, many connected the term with Jesus' call to make his disciples "fishers of men." Regardless of which of the three images the "fish" was connected with, there is no doubt that fish and fishing were strongly connected with Jesus and his followers.

Thinking of ourselves through the grid of being those who "fish for people" helps us to keep an eye on one of our chief tasks as God's servants. One of the significant responsibilities we have as believers is to catch other spiritual fish. That is, we are to share the love and word of Christ with those whom we have contact with in the prayer that God will use it to bring sinners to himself. Instead of this, however, many of us are simply "keepers of the aquarium" rather than fishers of people.[6]

When was the last time you threw your net out there in an everyday conversation? Are you regularly in the habit of casting out the net of the

---

6. The origin of the phrase "keepers of the aquarium" is often attributed to Paul Harvey, though this is debated.

Knowing Who You Are

good news or are you simply looking after your own fishbowl? While serving as a pastor I would sometimes have people in my congregation who would introduce me to workmates or family members who didn't know Christ with the hope that I would communicate the good news to them. While I was not averse to doing this, it seemed a little odd as the fellow believers knew their friends and family and were far more likely to have an impact in sharing the good news than I would. Don't depend on others to do your fishing. God has placed you in a part of the lake that you should be in. Drop your net, be patient, and let God work through you to draw other people to himself. Get fishing.

REFLECTIONS

1. Work can sometimes feel rewarding and at other times mundane. What is it in your labor for the Lord that requires perseverance?
2. Building requires a sturdy foundation. The foundation of the Christian life are the teachings of Jesus. How solid is your spiritual base? What can you be doing to build upon that foundation?
3. Fishing is a hard and sometimes lengthy endeavor. How would you rate your fishing for people at the moment? What have your learned or been reminded of by the ancient fisherman?
4. Write down the names and pray for some people you would like to see Jesus gather in.

PRAYER

> Creator God,
>
> Thank you that you have created us to work in your wonderful creation. We thank you for our jobs and the opportunities they present to reflect your creativity and goodness. Help us to be productive and reliable workers who delight in the tasks given us to us, whether spectacular or mundane. Like builders making wise decisions, give us insight into how to best follow your plans. Like fisherman, help us to cast the net so that others might be caught in the net of your grace and forgiveness. Grant us the willingness to serve joyfully in all circumstances, for Jesus' sake.
> Amen.

9

The Christian as Sheep

"I am the good shepherd; I know my sheep and my sheep know me."
—JOHN 10:14

> Jesus sought me when a stranger,
> Wandering from the fold of God;
> He, to rescue me from danger,
> Interposed His precious blood.
> —ROBERT ROBINSON, 1757

I AM A SPORTS devotee. It doesn't matter what the event, the code, or the discipline, I can guarantee that if it requires running, hitting, jumping, or kicking then I will happily invest my time in it. I'm just as happy watching a world cup soccer final as I am viewing seven-a-side rugby, cliff diving, basketball, or even curling. I love sport. *All* sport. There is just one thing I don't understand about sport, however, and that is the team "mascot." For years now I've often contemplated the team mascot. What is its purpose? Who chooses it? What is the criterion for selecting a mascot? Consider the diversity of the following mascots.

- The Newcastle *Knights*
- The Chicago *White Sox*

The Christian as Sheep

- The New South Wales *Waratahs*
- The Delhi *Daredevils*
- The Blackburn *Rovers*
- The South Sydney *Rabbitohs*
- The Miami *Heat*
- The Central *Cheetahs*

In the above list you have a variety of "mascots," from flowers such as the "Waratahs," to warring figures such as the "Knights." From climate conditions such as the "Heat," to entertaining "Daredevils." Apart from marketing value, why bother having a team "mascot" at all?

The word "mascot" can be traced back to a French word *mascotte* that was originally used of an ornament or icon that would bring about luck. During the 1800s in France if someone desired good fortune they would place a little *mascotte* in their home in the hope that the charm would generate prosperity. Obviously this practice was nothing more than superstition, but over time the idea of having a charm to represent one's luck shifted over to the sporting realm. Nowadays in the English language the term "mascot" has come to be synonymous with any object that symbolizes the purpose, character, or ideology of a particular society or group. The "mascot," I've ascertained, is a symbol designed to represent the ethos of the team and represent its character.

In the use of mascots far and away the most popular type are the animals. Team mascots such as the "bears," the "tigers," and the "crocodiles" are animals that encapsulate power and aggression, and are names given to represent strength and invoke fear in the opponents. Some mascots present a team as more savvy, crafty, and clever, such as the "hawks," the "taipans," and the "cheetahs." In a similar vein the authors of the New Testament also employed animals in various contexts as metaphors on how they should view themselves or others. Animals such as oxen, doves, snakes, hens, foxes, sparrows, pigs, ravens, goats, lambs, and fish are just some of those which are symbolically utilized to teach about life. Of the many animals that are representative of the people of God in the New Testament, however, the most common image for the people of God is the sheep.

CHRISTIANS ARE LIKE SHEEP

Sheep were important animals in the ancient world as they provided wool, milk, and meat for their owners. Sheep were endearing animals and often cherished as though they were members of the family.[1] Unlike the powerful lion, the majestic gazelle, or the wily rock-badger, sheep are by nature defenseless and in need of constant protection. Given their vulnerability and exposure to danger, it is apt that this animal came to symbolize God's people. In the Old Testament Israel are "the sheep" of God's "pasture" (Ps 79:13), and the "flock under his care" (Ps 95:7). When God picked a king to preside over his "flock" his choice was not a warrior, a politician, or a man of great esteem, but a humble *shepherd* boy (1 Sam 16:11). Though they had leaders to pastor them, however, ultimately Israel was to rely on the Lord as their "shepherd" (Ps 23:1).

The rich imagery of the people of God as "sheep" in the Old Testament is a theme that continues to unfold in the New Testament. In the midst of his ministry Jesus, when witnessing the masses of people, "had compassion on them, because they were like *sheep* without a shepherd" (Mark 6:34). But in what way are we like sheep? How are we similar to those crowded on the hills of Galilee? We are like sheep in that we *need a shepherd* because *we have a propensity to wander*.

Like Sheep We Need a Shepherd

Our natural disposition, like those in Jesus' audience, is that we are lost and vulnerable without his direction and protection. Sheep are generally gentle and placid animals. They are slow and not very agile, rendering them vulnerable to attack and in need of protection. It is easy to grasp how we are in this manner akin to sheep. Life is so often hard: the loss of a job, the death of a loved one, the confusion of a broken marriage. Often when hardships strike, like sheep we feel disoriented, vulnerable, and even abandoned. All of these things remind us that we have need of an advocate, a protector, and a shepherd.

Several years ago I discerned my need for a shepherd as I journeyed through the great the physical and emotional challenge of cancer. My wife and I were both devastated when I was diagnosed with a non-Hodgkin's lymphoma in my sinus. At the time I was serving as a pastor and we had

---

1. See, for example, 2 Sam 12:3–4.

just discovered that we were expecting our third child. Life was going smoothly until that Thursday night when the phone suddenly rang and a medical specialist brought our world crashing down.

The year that followed my diagnosis of cancer was crammed with endless appointments, extended stays in hospital, and all the nasty side effects that chemotherapy affords. The year was, in many ways, a blur. During this time I underwent a rollercoaster of emotions. I was anxious, confused, disappointed, sad, and uncertain. Like a sheep I felt exposed, endangered, and uncertain how to handle life. Fortunately for me, however, I had a shepherd who cared. As I searched the Scriptures, as I cried to God in prayer, and as I depended on God's people for encouragement and practical support, I found myself time and time again loved, sustained, and overwhelmed by God's grace. When the world was pulled out from under my feet I comprehended in a very real way that I was a sheep who needed help. I discovered how desperately I needed a shepherd.

I hope as you read this that you never have to deal with such extreme testing as cancer. The reality is, however, that in our broken world we will all experience some type of hardship or tragedy. There inevitably will come times, whether through illness, death, or loss, when we will feel vulnerable, exposed, isolated, and confused. At these times the weight of our mortality as well as inability to handle the hardships of life will come to the fore. When we encounter such crises we feel inadequate. We quickly discover that like a sheep we need a shepherd.

The challenge of being comparable to a sheep is that during our time of isolation and despair we often fail to remember that we have a "good shepherd." When a difficult time arises it is often easy to become overwhelmed and lose perspective of the big picture. Like sheep we are nervous, edgy, and uncertain. Remembering, however, that we have a good shepherd anchors us to reality. In the famous image of the Lord as our shepherd in Psalm 23, part of the comfort of the sheep lies in the fact that the shepherd is prepared with a "rod and staff." Whatever your trial, when you acknowledge that you are not alone, but have a good shepherd who oversees your soul, you can rest easy.

During one of the darkest times during my cancer treatment this truth came home in a resounding way. After going through a complicated medical procedure I found myself battling the difficult side effects. The net result of my harsh chemotherapy meant that I was bed-ridden for almost three long weeks. Being connected to various machines and being fed intravenously meant even something as simple as having a shower was hard work. One day after taking a shower I began to feel unwell and as I proceeded from the bathroom to my bed I suddenly blacked out, fainting to the ground. As I awoke doctors probed me with questions: "Who are you? What year is it? What is your date of birth?" At the same time the nurses scurried around the room busily searching for instruments to check my blood pressure. The medical team squeezed, poked, and prodded my body with all sorts of instruments. At this time I felt vulnerable, weak, and inadequate. I felt like a sheep.

My little fainting episode was obviously very disconcerting to my increasingly pregnant wife who was escorted out of the room. After I was stabilized the doctors informed us that they thought it best to relocate me to the intensive care unit so they could closely monitor me. As a patient, however, this was not good. Moving to ICU was not perceived as an upgrade but a downgrade. To shift to the ICU meant I was getting worse not better. I pleaded with the doctors to let me stay. My wife Tamara was clearly upset and had made up her mind that she would not vacate the hospital but would remain with me. We were both exhausted. In desperation we called out to God.

Shortly after, a gentle Polynesian doctor entered my room to check on me. He graciously agreed to personally assess me every two hours rather than requiring me to move to ICU. The doctor was very kind and his bedside manner was comforting. After he left my room I said to my wife, "that doctor must be a Christian. You can't be that nice and not a Christian." Two hours later the same doctor returned and said to me, "Mr Gill, I was looking through your hospital file and noticed you are a pastor." He continued, "I myself am a Christian, and I want to let you know that you are in much better hands than just the hospital's." I immediately burst into tears. God, our good shepherd, did indeed care for us. In our darkest valley God directed one of his children to remind us of his care. My wife returned home that evening and soundly slept knowing that the good shepherd was watching over us.

As sheep we are vulnerable and in constant need of attention and direction. The good news of the gospel is that we have a good shepherd who lays down his life for the sheep. This shepherd looks upon his people with compassion and tenderness (Mark 6:24). Jesus, our shepherd, is vigilant in his care and will never let us out of his sight. As he states:

> My sheep listen to my voice; I know them, and they follow me. I give them eternal life, and they shall never perish; no one will snatch them out of my hand. My Father, who has given them to me, is greater than all; no one can snatch them out of my Father's hand. (John 10:27-29)

When discouragement arises remember you have a shepherd. When financial difficulties threaten to undo you, remember you have a shepherd. When the dark valley of physical illness looms, remember you have a shepherd. Jesus has not, nor will he, abandon you. You are a tender sheep in the flock of God.

To consolidate the truth of God's shepherding heart I've found it helpful to commit to memory many of his great promises. More than once I've found myself lying in an MRI machine, or receiving an injection, or facing a fearful procedure and I've found that calling out to God and reminding him of his promises in Scripture brings comfort and peace. I've experienced a deep solace when I've mulled over in my mind the beauty and truth of God's word.

You may want to do the same. When going through the trial remind yourself that though you may be "considered as sheep to be slaughtered" (Rom 8:36) there is no experience that "will be able to separate us from the love of God that is in Christ Jesus our Lord" (Rom 8:39). Return to the truth that you have a "good shepherd" who "lays down his life for the sheep" (John 10:11). Remember that God has promised to "never leave you" or "forsake you" (Heb 13). The shepherd knows you and loves you. He will not abandon you his precious lamb.

So, like a sheep we need a shepherd, but there is a second thing we can observe and that is like sheep our propensity is to wander away from God.

Like Sheep Our Propensity Is to Wander

During my teenage years I lived in the unofficial "land of the sheep," the sleepy country of New Zealand. New Zealand is home to four million people and a staggering forty million sheep. Given the fact that there are around ten sheep to every person it should not be surprising to see sheep feature in much of New Zealand's day-to-day life. People in New Zealand wear "ugg boots," which are made from sheepskin. They produce their clothes from wool, which comes from sheep. The staple diet of the country is lamb, which is sheep. New Zealanders are keen about their fluffy white friends.

Knowing Who You Are

One of the clear indicators of New Zealand's fascination with sheep can be observed in the continued popularity of the 1980s and 90s television program, *A Dog Show*. This reality TV show followed the life of a working farm dog and its role in herding sheep. In this show the farmer and his faithful dog would labor together as they guided a flock of sheep up a steep grassy embankment with the goal of directing them through a narrow gate and finally into a pen. One hour of uninterrupted whistling, barking, and attention given to a flock of jumpy sheep. Riveting viewing! This show even had its own commentator who would reflect on the skill of the farmer, the speed of the dog, and, of course, the movement of the sheep.

Watching the herding of sheep was a great lesson particularly for someone who would later serve in pastoral ministry. Sheep, I observed, often traveled in packs and many times were unaware of where they were going. I also discovered that at any moment a sheep could suddenly flee the pack and bolt in the wrong direction. The shepherd, often with much frustration, would then leave the flock with the goal of retrieving the wandering sheep. Sometimes he would successfully restore the sheep to the flock, but just as often the sheep would refuse to cooperate. Sheep, I discovered, can be both delightful and frustrating at the same time.

While it was amusing to observe a sheep leave by tearing away from the flock, as someone who has served as a pastor I recognize that in the flock of God there is very little to laugh about when someone abandons their commitment to Christ and runs away from the fold. Sadly, over the years I've witnessed too many within the flock of God who have sought to feed in places outside of the shepherd's will. Some intentionally have left the flock lusting after money. Others have idealized leisure and prioritized personal happiness over costly discipleship. Still others have pursued immoral sexual relationships, gambling, or living for any of a number of futile and false gods. Other sheep I know have simply ambled off to the spiritual desert. While some sheep have been retrievable and have come back to the good shepherd, many choose not to come back. This is very sad.

If you've been a Christian for any length of time you will be able to identify people who have drifted from the faith: a mentor, a youth group leader, a work colleague, or a family member. Lest you and I get hasty in our judgment of these wayward sheep, however, we should recognize that within each of us is the impulse to leave the shepherd and to pursue life outside of God's supervision. As Isaiah reminds us, "we all, like sheep, have gone astray, each of us has turned to our own way" (Isa 53:6). Our natural default is to suppose we are sheep who can be sustained independently of the shepherd. Even those of us who know Christ still wrestle with the reality that our hearts and will often act in defiance of God. Many of us can relate to the words in the famous hymn *Come Thou Fount of Every Blessing* which states:

> O to grace how great a debtor daily I'm constrained to be
> Let thy goodness, like a fetter, bind my wandering heart to Thee.
> Prone to wander Lord I feel it, Prone to leave the God I love;
> Here's my heart O take and seal it, seal if for thy courts above.

Due to our depravity we are "prone to wander." As sheep it is imperative that we recognize this propensity and to make sure we regularly journey back to the shepherd of our souls.

As you read this you may be a sheep that has wandered. You may have absconded from God's fold in order to pursue what you thought would be happiness and significance, only to find yourself left feeling empty and disillusioned. The amazing news for you and me as wandering sheep is that we have a shepherd who will not simply let us go. Jesus spoke of this truth in a parable to his disciples.

> Suppose one of you has a hundred sheep and loses one of them. Doesn't he leave the ninety-nine in the open country and go after the lost sheep until he finds it? And when he finds it, he joyfully puts it on his shoulders and goes home. Then he calls his friends and neighbors together and says, "Rejoice with me; I have found my lost sheep." I tell you that in the same way there will be more rejoicing in heaven over one sinner who repents than over ninety-nine righteous persons who do not need to repent. (Luke 15:4–7)

This parable of Jesus is one of three stories given in Luke 15 that indicate how lost things can be found. In the context, Jesus was addressing the issue of the worth of "sinners" in the sight of God. Whereas some people assumed that there were individuals who were unfit to be loved by God, Jesus' point is that just as *every* sheep is important to the shepherd so also *every* lost or wandering person is loved and valued by God.

A few things stand out in Jesus' parable. The first is that even with a good shepherd there are sheep which get lost. We are not told why or how the sheep got lost only that it did. This sheep was no longer with the flock, so it was susceptible to all kinds of dangers, and it obviously didn't know where the flock was or it would have joined back in. Sheep can and do get lost. The propensity of the sheep to leave the flock is indicative of all our hearts before God. We are born with a natural desire where we think, foolishly, that we know more than the shepherd. As a result of our restless hearts we often find ourselves aimlessly meandering through life. We are confused, vulnerable, despairing, and often unaware of the dangers lurking about. Just as the sheep ambled away from the flock, so our nature is to do the same in relation to God.

We also see in this parable the love of the shepherd for the sheep. While the shepherd certainly cares for the ninety-nine his heart and mind are very much on rescuing the one that is lost. The good shepherd goes out into the field in search for the wandering sheep. He pursues the lost sheep because it belongs to him and is special to him. That is what a good shepherd does. Jesus exemplifies this type of shepherd when he said of himself:

> *I am the good shepherd. The good shepherd lays down his life for the sheep.* The hired hand is not the shepherd and does not own the sheep. So when he sees the wolf coming, he abandons the sheep and runs away. Then the wolf attacks the flock and scatters it. The man runs away because he is a hired hand and cares nothing for the sheep. *I am the good shepherd*; I know my sheep and my sheep know me— just as the Father knows me and I know the Father— and *I lay down my life for the sheep*. I have other sheep that are not of this sheep pen. I must bring them also. (John 10:14–16a)

In the ancient world the shepherd would make a pen for the sheep out of stones. The sheep would enter the pen and then the shepherd himself would lie across the entrance of the pen and act as the gate. In this way he physically "lay down" his life for the sheep. He kept the sheep in and the wolves out. But why would he risk himself in such a way? He did this because of his love for and commitment to the sheep.

In Jesus' parable of the lost sheep the shepherd puts himself in harm's way as he diligently searches for the lost one. He does so, not because he *needs* the sheep because he actually has ninety-nine others; rather, he does so because he has deep affection for the lost sheep. In a similar vein Jesus came to live among us as our shepherd in order that we, the restless, distracted, and often disobedient sheep, may come back to the fold of God. How much did it cost him? Jesus the great shepherd of the sheep loved his "flock" so much he bought it with "his own blood" (Acts 20:28). The good shepherd desperately cares for sheep that are wandering and lost.

The Christian as Sheep

The last thing to be observed in Jesus' parable is the response when the lost sheep is found. When the shepherd "finds it, he joyfully puts it on his shoulders and goes home" (Luke 15:5-6). This is a moving image. A tender, lost, dirty, confused, and vulnerable animal when located is hoisted upon the tired yet happy shoulders of the shepherd. Rather than the shepherd chastising the lost creature, the picture is one of relief and rejoicing. The shepherd doesn't immediately return to his flock, rather "he calls his friends and neighbors together and says, 'Rejoice with me; I have found my lost sheep'" (15:6). The shepherd is so pleased that his beloved lost sheep is found he rejoices and wants others to do so as well. The good shepherd is overjoyed because that which he loved is now home where it belongs.

The picture of Jesus the "good shepherd" finding the lost sheep gives great insight into the value God places on finding and restoring the lost sinner. The good news of the gospel is that no matter how far we roam from God, and we all have, Jesus the good shepherd pursues us with a love that knows no limit. When we, or other lost sinners, are rescued from our sin it is entirely appropriate to join the good shepherd and the heavenly hosts in songs of happiness.

The gospel is good news for us wandering sheep. Jesus doesn't abandon wandering sheep. He searches for and restores them. You may have committed adultery, you may have been dishonest in financial dealings, you may have been violent, rebellious, even blasphemous toward the things of Christ, yet in spite of that the good shepherd searches for you and calls you home. No matter what you've done, nothing can remove the shepherd's love for you, even if you've bolted from his flock. Again as the hymn writer penned:

> Jesus sought me when a stranger,
> Wandering from the fold of God;
> He, to rescue me from danger,
> Interposed His precious blood.

There are no sheep so lost that the great shepherd cannot find them. Drugs, a messy divorce, wayward living, an addiction to pornography, gambling, domestic violence, an abortion, whatever sins you may have committed the chief shepherd will not simply leave you. He pursues you today and seeks for you to come to the fold. The gospel reminds us that though our propensity is to wander, we have a loving shepherd who will rejoice in finding us.

Knowing Who You Are

REFLECTIONS

1. Like sheep we need a shepherd. In your experience when have been times when you have felt most vulnerable and abandoned? How did God shepherd you through that time?
2. Finish this sentence. "Good shepherd, right now I feel confused and disoriented about..."
3. As sheep our propensity is to wander. How did God find you and bring you into his fold? Share this with someone.
4. We have all strayed like sheep. Write down a list and pray for some lost sheep you know asking the good shepherd to bring them to his fold.

PRAYER

> Heavenly Father,
> Today I come to you as a needy and wayward sheep. In this confusing and broken world I've searched for meaning and significance in things other than you. I'm sorry for acting like an independent sheep. I need your protection, wisdom, and leading. Forgive me for choosing paths that lead to nowhere. I come to you as a wandering sheep asking that you would change my heart so that I may live for your Son's honor. Thank you for that "good shepherd" and the fact that he has laid down his life for me.
> Amen.

Bibliography

Augustine. *City of God*. Translated by George E. McCracken. LCL. Cambridge: Harvard University Press, 1957.
Bruce, F. F. "Citizenship." In *Anchor Bible Dictionary*, edited by David Noel Freeman, 1:1048–49. New York: Doubleday, 1992.
Bunyan, John. *The Complete Works of John Bunyan*. Philadelphia: Caxton, 1871.
Carmichael, Amy. *Gold Cord: The Story of a Fellowship*. Fort Washington: CLC, 1982.
Dio Chrysostom. *Discourses*. Translated by J. W. Cohoon. LCL. Cambridge: Harvard University Press, 1932.
Epictetus. *Discourses*. Translated by W. A. Oldfather. LCL. Cambridge: Harvard University Press, 1928.
Fantin, Joseph D. *The Lord of the Entire World*. Sheffield: Sheffield University Press, 2011.
Fee, Gordon. *The First Epistle to the Corinthians*. Grand Rapids: Eerdmans, 1987.
Hall, Douglas John. *The Steward: A Biblical Symbol Come of Age*. Grand Rapids: Eerdmans, 1990.
Hesiod. *Work and Days*. Translated by Glenn W. Most. LCL. Cambridge: Harvard University Press, 2006.
Hobbs, T. R. "War" in *Eerdmans Dictionary of the Bible*, edited by David Noel Freedman, 1365–66. Grand Rapids: Eerdmans, 2000.
Hoehner, Harold. *Ephesians: An Exegetical Commentary*. Grand Rapids: Baker, 2002.
Holmes, Michael, trans. *Martyrdom of Polycarp*. In *The Apostolic Fathers: Greek Texts and English Translations*, 226–48. 3rd ed. Grand Rapids: Baker Academic, 2007.
Jeffers, James S. *The Greco-Roman World of the New Testament Era*. Downers Grove: IVP, 1999.
Joachim Jeremias. *The Parables of Jesus*. London: SCM Press, 1963.
Josephus. *The Jewish War*. Translated by H. St. J. Thackeray. LCL. Cambridge University Press, 1928.
Judge, Edwin. *Social Distinctives of the Christians in the First Century: Pivotal Essays by E.A. Judge*. Edited by David Scholer. Peabody: Hendrickson, 2008.
Lewis, C. S. *The Lion, the Witch, and the Wardrobe*. New York: Harper Collins, 1994.
———. *The Weight of Glory and Other Addresses*. Grand Rapids: Eerdmans, 1965.
Livy. *Histories of Rome*. Translated by B. O. Foster. LCL. Cambridge: Harvard University Press, 1929.
Lucian. *Anarchis*. Translated by A. M. Harmon. LCL. Cambridge: Harvard University Press, 1925.
Lyall, Francis. *Slaves, Citizens, Sons: Legal Metaphors in the Epistles*. Grand Rapids: Zondervan, 1984.

Bibliography

MacArthur, John, Jr. *Slave: The Hidden Truth about Your Identity in Christ*. Nashville: Thomas Nelson, 2010.

McGrath, Alister. *The Journey: A Pilgrim in the Lands of the Spirit*. New York: Doubleday, 1999.

Philo. *The Contemplative Life*. Translated by F. H. Colson. LCL. Cambridge: Harvard University Press, 1967.

———. *The Worse Attacks the Better*. Translated by F. H. Colson and G. H. Whitaker. LCL. Cambridge: Harvard University Press, 1927.

Piper, John. *Don't Waste Your Life*. Wheaton: Crossway, 2003.

Pollock, John. *The Cambridge Seven*. Fearn: Christian Focus, 2006.

Polybius. *The Histories*. Translated by W. R. Paton. LCL. Cambridge: Harvard University Press, 1922.

Reumann, John. *Stewardship and the Economy of God*. Grand Rapids: Eerdmans, 1992.

Seneca. *Moral Epistles*. Translated by Richard M. Gummer. LCL. Cambridge: Harvard University Press, 1917–25.

Tacitus. *The Annals: Books XIII–XVI*. Translated by John Jackson. LCL. Cambridge: Harvard University Press, 2006.

Wilkins, Matthew. *Matthew*. Grand Rapids: Zondervan, 2004.

Winks, Joseph Foulkes. *The Christian Pioneer*. Leicester: Winks and Sons, 1856.

Xenophon. *Economics*. Translated by E. C. Marchant. LCL. Cambridge: Harvard University Press, 1923.

www.ingramcontent.com/pod-product-compliance
Lightning Source LLC
Chambersburg PA
CBHW071508150426
43191CB00009B/1448